Elsie R. Shore
Joseph R. Ferrari
Editors

Preventing Drunk Driving

Preventing Drunk Driving has been co-published simultaneously as *Journal of Prevention & Intervention in the Community*, Volume 17, Number 1 1998.

*Pre-publication
REVIEWS,
COMMENTARIES,
EVALUATIONS . . .*

"**A** rich array of new studies, which together illustrate the wide-ranging strategies needed to discourage driving after drinking. . . . Editors Elsie R. Shore and Joseph R. Ferrari have brought together several notable papers that help advance this cause."

William DeJong, PhD
*Lecturer
Harvard School
of Public Health
Boston, Massachusetts*

"There is no silver bullet when it comes to this battle to stamp out drunk driving in this country. The authors offer community activists examples of how to impact not only social drinkers but repeat offenders and all those in between. . . . A must read for anyone interested in reducing the needless injuries and death caused by the drunk driver."

Terrance D. Schiavone
President
National Commission
Against Drunk Driving
Washington, DC

The Haworth Press, Inc.

Preventing Drunk Driving

Preventing Drunk Driving has been co-published simultaneously as *Journal of Prevention & Intervention in the Community*, Volume 17, Number 1 1998.

The *Prevention & Intervention in the Community* Monographs/"Separates" (formerly the *Prevention in Human Services* series)*

Families as Nurturing Systems: Support Across the Life Span, edited by Donald G. Unger and Douglas R. Powell*

Religion and Prevention in Mental Health: Research, Vision, and Action, edited by Kenneth I. Pargament, Kenneth I. Maton, and Robert E. Hess*

Prevention and School Transitions, edited by Leonard A. Jason, Karen E. Danner, and Karen S. Kurasaki*

Self-Help and Mutual Aid Groups: International and Multicultural Perspectives, edited by Francine Lavoie, Thomasina Borkman, and Benjamin Gidron*

International Approaches to Prevention in Mental Health and Human Services, edited by Robert E. Hess and Wolfgang Stark*

Sexual Assault and Abuse: Sociocultural Context of Prevention, edited by Carolyn F. Swift*

Preventing Illness Among People with Coronary Heart Disease, edited by John D. Piette, Robert M. Kaplan, and Joseph R. Ferrari

Adolescent Health Care: Program Designs and Services, edited by John S. Wodarski, Marvin D. Feit, and Joseph R. Ferrari

Education in Community Psychology: Models for Graduate and Undergraduate Programs, edited by Clifford R. O'Donnell and Joseph R. Ferrari

Diversity Within the Homeless Population: Implications for Intervention, edited by Elizabeth M. Smith and Joseph R. Ferrari

Manhood Development in Urban African-American Communities, edited by Roderick J. Watts and Robert J. Jagers

Preventing Drunk Driving, edited by Elsie R. Shore and Joseph R. Ferrari

For information on previous issues of *Prevention in Human Services,* edited by Robert E. Hess, please contact: The Haworth Press, Inc., 10 Alice Street, Binghamton, NY 13904-1580 USA.

These books were published simultaneously as special thematic issues of *Journal of Prevention & Intervention in the Community* and are available bound separately. Visit Haworth's website at http://www.haworth.com to search our online catalog for complete tables of contents and ordering information for these and other publications. Or call 1-800-HAWORTH (outside US/Canada: 607-722-5857), Fax: 1-800-895-0582 (outside US/Canada: 607-771-0012), or e-mail getinfo@ haworth.com

Preventing Drunk Driving

Elsie R. Shore
Joseph R. Ferrari
Editors

Preventing Drunk Driving has been co-published simultaneously as *Journal of Prevention & Intervention in the Community,* Volume 17, Number 1 1998.

The Haworth Press, Inc.
New York • London

Preventing Drunk Driving has been co-published simultaneously as *Journal of Prevention & Intervention in the Community,* Volume 17, Number 1 1998.

The development, preparation, and publication of this work has been undertaken with great care. However, the publisher, employees, editors, and agents of The Haworth Press and all imprints of The Haworth Press, Inc., including The Haworth Medical Press and Pharmaceutical Products Press, are not responsible for any errors contained herein or for consequences that may ensue from use of materials or information contained in this work. Opinions expressed by the author(s) are not necessarily those of The Haworth Press, Inc.

Cover design by Thomas J. Mayshock Jr.

The Haworth Press, Inc., 10 Alice Street, Binghamton, NY 13904-1580 USA

Library of Congress Cataloging-in-Publication Data

Preventing drunk driving / Elsie R. Shore, Joseph R. Ferrari, editors.
    p. cm.
    Published also as v. 17, no. 1, 1998 of the Journal of prevention & intervention in the community.
    Includes bibliographical references and index.
    ISBN 0-7890-0511-5
    1. Drunk Driving–Prevention.   I. Ferrari, Joseph R. II. Journal of prevention & intervention in the community.
HE5620.D7P83 1998
363.12′514–dc21
                                         98-12120
                                         CIP

INDEXING & ABSTRACTING

Contributions to this publication are selectively indexed or abstracted in print, electronic, online, or CD-ROM version(s) of the reference tools and information services listed below. This list is current as of the copyright date of this publication. See the end of this section for additional notes.

- *Abstracts of Research in Pastoral Care & Counseling*, Loyola College, 7135 Minstrel Way, Suite 101, Columbia, MD 21045
- *Behavioral Medicine Abstracts,* University of Washington, Department of Social Work & Speech & Hearing Sciences, Box 354900, Seattle, WA 98195
- *Child Development Abstracts & Bibliography*, University of Kansas, 213 Bailey Hall, Lawrence, KS 66045
- *CNPIEC Reference Guide: Chinese National Directory of Foreign Periodicals*, P.O. Box 88, Beijing, Peoples Republic of China
- *Excerpta Medica/Secondary Publishing Division*, Elsevier Science Inc., Secondary Publishing Division, 655 Avenue of the Americas, New York, NY 10010
- *Family Studies Database (online and CD/ROM),* National Information Services Corporation, 306 East Baltimore Pike, 2nd Floor, Media, PA 19063
- *HealthPromis*, Health Education Authority (HEA)/Health Promotion Information Centre, Hamilton House-Mabledon Place, London WC1H 9TX, England
- *IBZ International Bibliography of Periodical Literature,* Zeller Verlag GmbH & Co., P.O.B. 1949, d-49009 Osnabruck, Germany
- *INTERNET ACCESS (& additional networks) Bulletin Board for Libraries ("BUBL"), coverage of information resources on INTERNET, JANET, and other networks.*
  - <URL:http://bubl.ac.uk/>
  - The new locations will be found under <URL:http://bubl.ac. uk/link/>.
  - Any existing BUBL users who have problems finding information on the new service should contact the BUBL help line by sending e-mail to <bubl@bubl.ac.uk>.
  The Andersonian Library, Curran Building, 101 St. James Road, Glasgow G4 0NS, Scotland
- *Mental Health Abstracts (online through DIALOG)*, IFI/Plenum Data Company, 3202 Kirkwood Highway, Wilmington, DE 19808
- *National Clearinghouse on Child Abuse & Neglect,* 10530 Rosehaven Street, Suite 400, Fairfax, VA 22030-2804
- *NIAAA Alcohol and Alcohol Problems Science Database (ETOH),* National Institute on Alcohol Abuse and Alcoholism, 1400 Eye Street NW, Suite 600, Washington, DC 20005
- *OT BibSys,* American Occupational Therapy Foundation, P.O. Box 31220, Rockville, MD 20824-1220

(continued)

- *Referativnyi Zhurnal (Abstracts Journal of the All-Russian Institute of Scientific and Technical Information)*, 20 Usievich Street, Moscow 125219, Russia
- *RMDB DATABASE (Reliance Medical Information)*, Reliance Medical Information, Inc. (RMI), 100 Putnam Green, Greenwich, CT 06830
- *Social Planning/Policy & Development Abstracts (SOPODA)*, Sociological Abstracts, Inc., P. O. Box 22206, San Diego, CA 92192-0206
- *Social Work Abstracts*, National Association of Social Workers, 750 First Street NW, 8th Floor, Washington, DC 20002
- *Sociological Abstracts (SA)*, Sociological Abstracts, Inc., P. O. Box 22206, San Diego, CA 92192-0206
- *SOMED (social medicine) Database*, Landes Institut fur Den Offentlichen Gesundheitsdienst NRW, Postfach 20 10 12, D-33548 Bielefeld, Germany
- *Violence and Abuse Abstracts: A Review of Current Literature on Interpersonal Violence (VAA)*, Sage Publications, Inc., 2455 Teller Road, Newbury Park, CA 91320

SPECIAL BIBLIOGRAPHIC NOTES

related to special journal issues (separates)
and indexing/abstracting

☐ indexing/abstracting services in this list will also cover material in any "separate" that is co-published simultaneously with Haworth's special thematic journal issue or DocuSerial. Indexing/abstracting usually covers material at the article/chapter level.

☐ monographic co-editions are intended for either non-subscribers or libraries which intend to purchase a second copy for their circulating collections.

☐ monographic co-editions are reported to all jobbers/wholesalers/approval plans. The source journal is listed as the "series" to assist the prevention of duplicate purchasing in the same manner utilized for books-in-series.

☐ to facilitate user/access services all indexing/abstracting services are encouraged to utilize the co-indexing entry note indicated at the bottom of the first page of each article/chapter/contribution.

☐ this is intended to assist a library user of any reference tool (whether print, electronic, online, or CD-ROM) to locate the monographic version if the library has purchased this version but not a subscription to the source journal.

☐ individual articles/chapters in any Haworth publication are also available through the Haworth Document Delivery Service (HDDS).

Preventing Drunk Driving

CONTENTS

ABOUT THE EDITORS

Elsie R. Shore, PhD, is Professor of Psychology at Wichita State University in Wichita, Kansas. Dr. Shore conducts research on the prevention of drunk driving and on women and alcohol. She has received grants from the National Institute on Alcohol Abuse and Alcoholism, the National Commission Against Drunk Driving, and the Fund for the Improvement of Post-Secondary Education. She also coordinates the Substance Abuse Counselor Training Curriculum at Wichita State University.

Joseph R. Ferrari, PhD, is Visiting Assistant Professor in the Department of Psychology at DePaul University in Chicago, Illinois, and Editor-in-Chief of the *Journal of Prevention & Intervention in the Community.* Dr. Ferrari received his PhD from Adelphi University, with a concentration in experimental social-personality psychology. In addition to his interest in mainstream social psychological issues, such as persuasion, attribution theory, and altruism, he has developed several lines of research in social-community psychology. His community research includes the psychological sense of community, caregiver stress and satisfaction, community service, and behavior analysis applications to community issues.

Foreword

The National Highway Traffic Safety Administration (NHTSA) reports that there has been a 24 percent reduction in the number of alcohol-related auto crash fatalities in 1995, as compared to 1985. Nevertheless, in 1995 there were 17,274 such alcohol-related deaths, representing 41 percent of all traffic fatalities (NHTSA, 1996a). Drivers 15 to 20 years old experienced the largest decline in involvement in fatal crashes during this period. This encouraging finding is tempered, however, by the fact that more than three thousand young drivers were killed and over 4,600 injured in 1995; 20 percent of these young people were intoxicated at the time of the crash, despite the fact that drinking under the age of 21 is illegal in every state in the United States (NHTSA, 1996b).

Recognition of drunk driving as a public health and safety problem is relatively recent. The now-classic first studies demonstrating a link between alcohol use and impaired driving appeared in the 1970s. Interest in the issue remained low until the 1980s, when public awareness and media attention greatly increased. Government involvement and research, prevention, and intervention efforts also increased during that period.

The history and range of efforts directed at the prevention of drunk driving could serve as a handbook for students of prevention. Grass-roots organizations such as Mothers Against Drunk Driving (MADD) have had a significant impact, primarily by lobbying for stricter laws and swifter and more certain apprehension and punishment, but also by informing the public of the extent and costs of the problem. Evaluations of the effects of changes in drunk driving laws demonstrate both the preventive benefits of legal sanctions and their limitations. When legal sanctions proved not to be the cure-all,

[Haworth co-indexing entry note]: "Foreword." Shore, Elsie. Co-published simultaneously in *Journal of Prevention & Intervention in the Community* (The Haworth Press, Inc.) Vol. 17, No. 1, 1998, pp. xi-xii; and: *Preventing Drunk Driving* (ed: Elsie R. Shore, and Joseph R. Ferrari) The Haworth Press, Inc., 1998, pp. xi-xii. Single or multiple copies of this article are available for a fee from The Haworth Document Delivery Service [1-800-342-9678, 9:00 a.m. - 5:00 p.m. (EST). E-mail address: getinfo@haworth.com].

xi

other approaches were developed. Server training and designated driver programs seek to involve friends, family, and others in prevention; ride service programs give the impaired person an alternative to driving. Passengers are receiving attention not only as potential intervenors but also as targets for programs encouraging them to refuse to ride with an impaired person.

Another part of the effort has been directed at secondary prevention, trying to find ways to reduce drunk driving recidivism. These efforts include education programs for adjudicated drunk drivers, the use of monitoring programs and alternatives to incarceration, and the alteration of the vehicle so that it cannot be driven by an alcohol-impaired person. Determining whether the offender is in need of treatment for substance dependence/alcoholism or is non-addicted and in need of other forms of intervention is yet another aspect of the work. Finally, of course, the effectiveness of the variety of treatments and other interventions must be assessed.

This volume cannot be that handbook of drunk driving prevention. It does, however, provide a sample of some of the work presently being done in the field. Even with the space limitations of this volume, the range of activity is obvious. The researchers presented here are looking at ways to increase designated driver behavior, to provide drinkers with feedback about their level of intoxication, and to identify potential recidivists. They are developing theoretical models of drunk driving intervention behavior, assessing the usefulness of vehicle interlock programs, and using mapping to target prevention activities to those most at risk. It is hoped that this array will provide the reader with some sense both of the need for this work and of its richness.

Elsie R. Shore
Department of Psychology
Wichita State University

REFERENCES

National Highway Traffic Safety Administration. *Traffic Safety Facts 1995: Overview.* Washington, D.C.: U.S. Department of Transportation, 1996a.
National Highway Traffic Safety Administration. *Traffic Safety Facts 1995: Young Drivers.* Washington, D.C.: U.S. Department of Transportation, 1996b.

Analyzing Methods
for Increasing Designated Driving

Steven E. Meier

University of Idaho

Thomas Armon Brigham
Bo James Gilbert

Washington State University

SUMMARY. A designated driver is an individual who abstains from consuming alcohol and is available to drive home companions who have been drinking. Although increasing designated driving may help reduce the frequency of driving while intoxicated, few empirical studies have been done on designated driving. As a consequence, little is known about the actual numbers of designated drivers at drinking establishments or how to increase that frequency. This paper reports on three experiments designed to test methods for increasing participation in designated driving programs at drinking establishments. The results are analyzed in terms of their implications for the role designated driving programs might play in reducing the frequency of driving while intoxicated behavior. *[Article copies available for a fee from The Haworth Document Delivery Service: 1-800-342-9678. E-mail address: getinfo@haworth.com]*

Address correspondence to T.A. Brigham at the Department of Psychology, Washington State University, Pullman, WA 99164-4820.

This research was supported by a contract from the Washington Traffic Safety Commission to T.A. Brigham, principal investigator.

[Haworth co-indexing entry note]: "Analyzing Methods for Increasing Designated Driving." Meier, Steven E., Thomas Armon Brigham, and Bo James Gilbert. Co-published simultaneously in *Journal of Prevention & Intervention in the Community* (The Haworth Press, Inc.) Vol. 17, No. 1, 1998, pp. 1-14; and: *Preventing Drunk Driving* (ed: Elsie R. Shore, and Joseph R. Ferrari) The Haworth Press, Inc., 1998, pp. 1-14. Single or multiple copies of this article are available for a fee from The Haworth Document Delivery Service [1-800-342-9678, 9:00 a.m. - 5:00 p.m. (EST). E-mail address: getinfo@haworth.com].

1

Considerable evidence indicates that Driving While Intoxicated (DWI) remains a serious social problem. Although gradual reductions in DWI have occurred over the past 10 years, national reports show that 41% of all traffic fatalities in 1994 involved an alcohol intoxicated or alcohol impaired individual (CDC, 1995). To date, the main approach for dealing with driving while intoxicated has been to suppress the behavior through increased legal sanctions and increased enforcement efforts. Recently, however, there appears to have been an increase in the level of intoxicated driving fatalities (NHTSA, 1996) suggesting that additional interventions may be needed. In this regard, educational and social procedures may be useful in reducing the prevalence of DWI and related auto fatalities.

Designated driving is one form of prosocial behavior that could possibly contribute to this effort. Designated drivers are individuals within a group of alcohol consumers who abstain from alcohol during a particular drinking occasion. This person then chauffeurs the drinking individuals to their place of residence after the drinking occasion has ended. Logically, increasing designated driving should directly and proportionately reduce the numbers of alcohol impaired drivers leaving a drinking establishment or party. Thus, designated driving has received considerable attention in the press (Johnson, 1995) and has been advocated by some policy makers (e.g., Apsler, Harding, and Goldfein, 1987; Johnson, 1995). It has also been promoted and sponsored by brewers (e.g., Anheuser-Busch). It is also not surprising that designated driving has generated some controversy. For example, critics such as DeJong and Wallack suggest that designated driver programs encourage other group members to over consume and ultimately detract from other enforcement efforts. However, despite the general interest and debate concerning designated driving, few systematic studies have been conducted on the topic. Indeed, several authors (Apsler et al., 1987; DeJong & Wallack, 1992; Shore, Gregory, & Tatlock, 1991; Wagenaar, 1992) have commented on the extreme paucity of empirical studies of designated driving and its effects.

The first systematic experimental study of methods to increase designated driving was published by Brigham, Meier, and Goodner (1995). In that study, low frequencies of designated driving at a drinking establishment were increased and the intervention evaluated using a reversal design. The intervention consisted of an incentive program that provided free nonalcoholic beverages including nonalcoholic beers and wines in addition to the standard soft drinks and coffee. It was reasoned that designated drivers would feel more comfortable and be less discriminable to their drinking friends if they had a glass of nonalcoholic beer or wine rather than a soft drink. The program was described on large 70mm by 100mm posters strategically placed around the bar. The posters also instructed patrons to tell their server if they had a designated driver. The research demonstrated that it was possible to significantly increase the frequency of designated driving and suggested that similar procedures might be used to develop community wide designated driving programs.

There were, however, a number of limitations to this study. First, it involved only a single bar catering primarily to college students and other young adults in a rural community. Could the procedures be replicated in other settings involving different populations? Second, potential designated drivers learned about the intervention mainly through on the premise advertising. Would more people decide to become designated drivers if the program were more widely known? A series of experiments were designed to examine these issues. The first experiment was a systematic replication of Brigham et al. (1995) in two college communities with the addition of an advertising campaign in the respective college newspapers. Experiment 2 was conducted in a much larger city and was an effort to see if designated driving would appeal to a broader population. The final experiment tested the effectiveness of cable television advertising.

EXPERIMENT 1

Method

Setting. This experiment was conducted in two university communities in the western United States at two bars that catered to college students and other young adults with the majority of patrons falling in the 21 to 35 age range. The bars both offered food service, occasional live music and dancing, and generally fit the profile of a college night spot. Both bars had participated in alcohol related research with the authors in the past (see Brigham et al., 1995; Meier, Brigham Ward, Myers, & Warren, 1996).

Observational Procedures. The observational procedures used in this experiment were the same as those developed for the Brigham et al. (1995) study. For the present experiment, an advanced graduate research assistant first trained and then supervised 30 undergraduates who served as observers. In order to recognize and observe designated drivers, a designated driver was defined as a person who identifies himself/herself to the server as a designated driver and asks to participate in the program. As part of the bars' participation in the program, servers were to contact the observers and point out the designated driver. However, because the servers often became very busy, the observers were also taught to periodically ask servers if anyone had self-identified as a designated driver and to observe the bartender for the preparation of nonalcoholic drinks. In addition, because drinks for designated drivers were marked as free on the order slips, bartenders were asked to signal the observers when an order was received from a designated driver. Finally, the bar managers were very committed to the program and regularly reminded their staffs of the importance of cooperating with the observers.

Teams of three trained undergraduates were then assigned on a rotating basis to observe designated drivers in each bar. The observer teams arrived at their assigned bar at approximately 8:30 pm, began observing at 9:00 pm, and terminated observations at 12:30 am. After arriving, they introduced themselves to the servers and bartenders. The observers were stationed near the bartender to make it easier for a server or the bartender to indicate when they had a designated driver drink order. When the observers received a cue from either a server or bartender, one observer followed the server to identify the designated driver and count the number of people in the group. Once the designated driver was identified, the person was periodically observed during the evening to determine if alcoholic beverages were consumed by the individual. Finally, when the group left the bar, two observers unobtrusively followed to determine if the individual did in fact drive the group from the premises.

Over the course of the experiment, five individuals purporting to be designated drivers did not drive and were removed from the count of designated drivers.

In addition to the regular observers, two pairs of reliability observers were separately trained. They were then introduced to the managers and bartenders. The regular observers were not aware of the reliability observers or that they would periodically check the accuracy of the regular observers' reports. Reliability observers were required to arrive at the assigned bar no later than 8:15 to check in with the manager and the bartender. They then checked all of the activities of the regular observation team including their time of arrival, when they began observing, etc. A total of 10 reliability checks were conducted with the resulting reliability .93.

Experimental Design. The research used a group replication design with a repeated measures design which is similar to the multiple time series design described by Campbell and Stanley (1963). It also resembles a multiple baseline design (Baer, Wolf & Risely, 1968) but the introduction of the independent variable is based on the passage of a set time period rather than the stability of the baselines. The baseline and intervention phases each lasted 9 evenings, however, data collection did not begin in Bar 2 until data had been collected for three evenings in Bar 1.

Intervention. The experimental manipulation consisted of two components, an incentive program to encourage and reward designated driving and a print advertising campaign publicizing the availability of the designated driving program at a particular bar. The ads were large 9.5 cm by 12.5 cm and were run in respective university newspapers on Wednesdays and Fridays. The text of the advertisement was as follows, "Free drink and munchies! Wednesday, Friday, and Saturday at Name of Bar. When you are a *Designated Driver* you will receive: Free non-alcoholic beer and soft drinks plus a basket of chips and salsa and a coupon for $3 off a pitcher of beer on your next visit. Present this ad to your server between 9 p.m. and midnight to participate. Minimum age is 21." As with most programs requiring a participant to present an ad to participate, copies of the ads were available in the bars for people who did not have one.

Results and Discussion. As shown in Table 1, there was a clear increase in designated driving in Bar 2 after the introduction of the advertisements and incentive program ($t(8) = 6.183$, $p < .001$). In Bar 1, a slight increase in designated driving occurred after the intervention, but it was not significant ($t(8) = .978$, $p = .35$). It is unclear why the intervention appeared to work at one bar but not the other. The first bar had higher baseline levels of designated driving, and it was expected the advertisements would produce a proportionate increase in this level. However, the increase did not occur. On the other hand, the advertisements were associated with an increase in designated driving in Bar 2 where the baseline was much lower. Comparisons of clientele, weather, enforcement activities, and other variables produced no obvious explanations.

One possibility worthy of further analysis is the idea of a ceiling effect. In any particular bar, there may be a limited number of candidates to become designated drivers, i.e., people drinking in groups of three or more. If for some reason a high proportion of them are already designated drivers, then an intervention can have little effect.

EXPERIMENT 2

This experiment was a systematic replication of Experiment 1, but was conducted in a much larger neighboring city with an urban-suburban population of approximately 400,000. The area was selected because college students made up a significantly smaller percentage of the young adult population in comparison to the earlier studies. These differences were considered important in determining whether designated driving was a viable alternative for young adults in general, rather than solely for college students in a university community.

TABLE 1. A Comparison of Designated Driver Behavior in Two University Bars

	Bar 1	Bar 2
Baseline		
Mean Number of Designated Drivers	2.22	1.0
Range	0-4	0-2
Treatment		
Mean Number of Designated Drivers	3.0	4.22
Range	0-7	0-6

Setting. The two bars participating in this study were considerably different from those in Experiment 1 and from each other. Bar 1 was an upscale downtown restaurant and bar catering primarily to a young professional crowd. The bar section featured a pool/billiard table, multiple televisions, and a large screen television. The second bar was a much larger establishment featuring live bands playing mainly country rock. This bar attracted large crowds with the activity centered around dancing and drinking.

Observational Procedures. Training, observers, and observational procedures were essentially the same as those in Experiment 1. The main difference was that the observers were undergraduates recruited with the assistance of a colleague from a local university. In addition, a second graduate assistant who lived in the city was hired to help train and supervise the observers. All of the critical procedures remained the same.

Experimental Design. Experiment 2 used the same group replication design as Experiment 1, with the minor change that baselines and interventions were four weeks long, instead of three weeks long.

Intervention. Again, the same set of incentives and advertising programs were used. In this study, the advertisements were run in the sports section of the city's major newspaper.

Results and Discussion. These results were remarkably similar to those in Experiment 1 and are presented in Table 2. That is, a significant designated driving increase occurred in Bar 1 where the baseline was very low ($t(11) = 3.188$, $p < .01$). Similarly, there was no significant change in Bar 2, where baseline level was far higher ($t(11) = .422$, $p < .68$). These results tend to support the ceiling effect hypothesis put forward earlier. However, a second possible explanation for the lack of change in Bar 2 is that the patrons of this establishment were not careful newspaper readers. A spot check of this bar found that few individuals recalled seeing the advertisements. This observation suggests that print advertising may not be an effective method for communicating with these young adults.

There is, however, an additional point to be made about the results of this study. Overall, the level of designated driving in the "Country and Western bar" was quite high throughout the observation period. Typically, designated driving is not thought to be part of

TABLE 2. A Comparison of Designated Driver Behavior in Two Urban Bars

	Bar 1	Bar 2
Baseline		
Mean Number of Designated Drivers	.667	6.33
Range	0-2	2-10
Treatment		
Mean Number of Designated Drivers	1.583	6.583
Range	0-3	3-10

this bar scene. Thus, it was considered promising to discover the high frequency of designated driving with this clientele and suggests that designated driving can be attractive to a broad range of young adults.

EXPERIMENT 3

After Experiment 2, a spot check of patrons suggested that very few actually were aware of the newspaper advertisements or the designated driver program in the bars. It was hypothesized that the varied response to the designated driver program was not due to a lack of interest in designated driving, but due to a lack of general information about the program. Further investigation suggested that young adults were more likely to watch such cable television channels as ESPN, CNN, USA, and MTV rather than to read newspapers. Experiment 3 was then designed to test the effectiveness of cable television advertisements as a method for increasing the numbers of designated drivers at a particular bar.

On this basis, it was decided to develop a television advertisement for the designated driving program and present it on an urban cable television system. Because of the research and public interest aspects of the project, when approached, the cable system agreed to run the advertisements at a reduced rate. It was felt that the advertisement would have to be very upbeat, exciting, and salient so that it would catch the viewers' attention. Further, the advertisement should emphasize the positive aspects of being a designated driver. Intuitively, it was thought that these would be important elements in influencing an individual's decision to become a designated driver.

After polling several classes on what they thought would make a good ad and appeal to young adults, the spot was modeled on a game show. A group of patrons are shown entering the bar. A waitress begins taking their orders, and the third customer states, "He is the designated driver tonight." The waitress then blows a whistle and announces to the entire bar, "We have a winner." Everyone else in the bar stands up and applauds. Again following the game show model, the waitress loudly asks, "Tell me Jerry, what has he (she) won?" The manager then describes the designated driver program as if it were a prize. The ad then ends with the statements, "Everybody is a winner when you are a designated driver" and "Have a good time–Be responsible." Although the advertisement was not pilot tested before it was run, students in the same classes were very enthusiastic about it.

Setting. The experiment was conducted at the same urban Bar 1 of Experiment 2. This bar was selected because the entire staff (manager, bartenders, and servers) were very positive and cooperative with the earlier study. Furthermore, the establishment had developed a very systematic and accurate set of procedures for tracking the number of designated drivers. As a consequence, it was not necessary to have university observers there every evening to check their count, but three reliability checks were run during each phase of the experiment. Finally, they were very enthusiastic about having an advertisement filmed at their establishment and run on local television.

Experimental Design. Because a single bar was involved in this study, an ABA reversal design was used. In this design, three weeks of baseline data were collected (A), the advertisements and incentive program were introduced for three weeks (B), the ads and incentives were then withdrawn followed by a second three week baseline (A).

Intervention. The intervention consisted of the incentive program used in Experiments 1 and 2 plus the cable television advertisements announcing the incentive program and inviting people to be a designated driver at the establishment. The intervention lasted three weeks and during that period the advertisement ran approximately 200 times.

Results and Discussion. The introduction of the intervention had a clear and statistically significant impact on the number of designated drivers. The results are presented in Table 3. The mean num-

TABLE 3. An Analysis of Television Advertisements in an Urban Drinking Establishment

	Baseline 1	Treatment	Baseline
Mean Number of Designated Drivers	.333	4.11	.333
Range	0-1	2-6	0-1

ber of designated drivers per night during the two baseline periods was 0.333, while the mean increased to 4.11 during the intervention. Statistical comparisons of the results of the two baselines with those of the intervention were significant at the .001 level ($t(8) = 3.778, p < .001$) and ($t(8) = 3.778, p < .001$).

Perhaps an equally important and completely unpredicted result was that the bar experienced a 350% increase in the sales of nonalcoholic beverages (e.g., "O'Douls") during the intervention period. The manager further reported he and his staff felt the "atmosphere" in the bar was more positive and relaxed during the intervention. This, of course, is a subjective judgment without any objective data to support it. Nonetheless, it was made by a highly experienced and professional staff. Clearly, these were unexpected results that may be side effects of the intervention, but more research is needed to verify this possible relationship.

Irrespective of their anecdotal nature, the manager's observations tend to contradict the often heard criticism of designated driving that it promotes binge drinking by the riders (see Johnson, 1995 for a full discussion of this issue). People overconsuming alcohol are often loud and disruptive and certainly would not contribute to the relaxed atmosphere correlated with the increase in designated driving. In fact, it has been our experience in this research program that groups with clearly identified designated drivers simply do not behave in a disorderly fashion. These observations, informal though they may be, are consistent with the findings of other researchers who are reporting the absence of a major binge drinking effect with designated driving (e.g., Winsten, 1995). Further, it appears that under conditions like those in the present research that a designated driver may actually have a moderating effect on the drinking of the other group members. As Winsten notes, "We hear anecdotally that the sober person at the table, to a degree, serves as a brake on the drinking of others" (as cited in Johnson, 1995). Again, systematic research is required to determine the conditions under which this effect may occur. Nonetheless, these observations suggest that predicting having a sober designated driver will have a moderating influence on the drinking of the other group members is at least as plausible as the license to drink hypothesis.

GENERAL CONCLUSIONS

The present paper has presented three experiments designed to increase designated driving. Taken in conjunction with other research, the results of these studies indicate that designated driving can be increased. The question then arises as to whether the return in terms of increased designated driving justifies the effort required to produce it. For instance, in Experiment 3, the number of designated drivers was increased from less than one a night to over four per night, but an extensive and expensive advertising and incentive program was required to produce those gains. This apparently modest return leads to at least two questions. First, why weren't there more substantial increases in the frequency of designated driving? At present, there is no certain answer to this question, but one logical possibility is that there is a natural ceiling effect on the number of potential designated drivers. Although it is possible for one person in a couple to be the designated driver, this only occurred twice in the experiments reported here. Therefore, designated driving as measured in this research functionally only occurs in groups of three or more people. In the bars where the research was conducted, the vast majority of patrons came as either singles or pairs. As a consequence, at any time, there was a limited number of groups where it was possible for someone to become a designated driver. Because people mingle, it is difficult to establish with certainty the number of groups and their composition in a crowded bar. However, in Experiment 3, it was estimated that the number of groups of three or more people in the bar ranged from six to thirteen per night with a median of eight. As a consequence, a more accurate way of representing the results might be that designated driving was increased from less than 5% of the available population to approximately 50% of that population. Thus, the results can be seen as quite substantial. Nonetheless, the focus of future research will be to determine what steps are required to further increase the percentage of groups participating in designated driver programs.

A second and clearly related question is: Are the gains in designated driving worth the effort? Again, there is no definitive answer to the question, but there are a number of reasons why a community might wish to invest in a designated driving program. The first reason is the numbers of potential impaired drivers affected. In the present research, the median size of groups with a designated driver was four people. This means that every designated driver substantially reduced the number of people who might drive after drinking. Recent data from the National Highway Traffic Safety Administration (1995) show that these people represent an important part of the driving under the influence problem. When 600 people who admitted driving a vehicle when impaired were interviewed, a significant portion reported either driving while impaired or riding with an impaired driver because there was no sober individual available to act as the designated driver. Thus, designated driving has a multiplicative effect in reducing the numbers of impaired drivers.

A second and slightly more subtle reason is that designated driving is a prosocial behavior. The designated driver is doing something for the good of the larger group. Such positive social behavior seems like an activity that the community would wish to encourage for the betterment of all.

Finally, based on the present research, it appears that designated driving has the potential to play an important role in community wide efforts to reduce the frequency of DWI and alcohol related traffic accidents. Along these lines, Holder (1993) and Voas (1997) have argued that increased enforcement efforts alone have probably reached their maximum level of effectiveness, and additional strategies will be required for further progress. They have called for multicomponent community wide programs and have suggested that some of the components should have some positive elements that the entire community can endorse and get behind. Given the enthusiastic response of bar owners and managers to the designated driver research and the positive reactions in local newspapers, designated driving programs certainly could play such a role.

If designated driving is to have a more important role, the focus of advertising, educational, and incentive programs should be to "normalize" the practice. Normalize in this case means the behavior is the expected norm. For instance, an important step in the battle against AIDS in the gay community was the effort to make the regular use of condoms the expected norm in the community (e.g., Kelly, St. Lawrence, Brasfield, Lemke, Amedei, Roffman, Hood, Smith, Kilgore, & McNeil, 1990). A similar effort is needed to make the selection of a designated driver when groups go out to drink the standard practice. In this regard, the finding that many young adults have been designated drivers (Johnson, 1995) and the observation of a substantial number of designated drivers at a country and western bar are encouraging. Nonetheless, a more systematic and community wide effort is required if this fairly common behavior is to be transformed into the expected norm. In conclusion, designated driving has the potential to make a significant contribution to quality of life in our communities and should be strongly supported.

REFERENCES

Apsler, R., Harding, W., & Goldfein, J. (1987). The review and assessment of designated driver programs as an alcohol countermeasure approach. *U.S. Department of Transportation, National Highway Traffic Safety Administration.* DOT HS 807 108. pp. 1-40.

Baer, D.M., Wolf, M.M., & Risley, T.R. (1968). Some current dimensions of applied behavior analysis. *Journal of Applied Behavior Analysis, 1,* 91-97.

Brigham, T. A., Meier, S. E., & Goodner, V. (1995). Increasing the frequency of designated driving with a program of prompts and incentives. *Journal of Applied Behavior Analysis, 28,* 83-85.

Campbell, D.T., & Stanley, J.C. (1963). *Experimental and Quasi-Experimental Designs for Research.* Chicago: McNally.

Centers for Disease Control and Prevention (1995). Alcohol involvement in fatal motor-vehicle crashes–United States, 1993-1994. *Morbidity and Mortality Weekly Report, 44,* 886-887.

DeJong, W., & Wallack, L. (1992). The role of designated driver programs in the prevention of alcohol-impaired driving: A critical reassessment. *Health Education Quarterly, 19,* 429-442.

Holder, H.D. (1993). Prevention of alcohol-related accidents in the community. *Addiction, 88,* 1003-1012.

Johnson, E. (1995). Cheers to the designated driver. *Traffic Safety, 95,* 6-11.

Kelly, J., St. Lawrence, J., Brasfield, T., Lemke, A., Amedei, T., Roffman, R., Hood, H., Smith, J., Kilgore, H., & McNeil, C. (1990). Psychological factors that predict AIDS precautionary behavior. *Journal of Consulting and Clinical Psychology, 58,* 117- 120.

Meier, S. E., Brigham, T. A., Ward, D. A., Myers, F., & Warren, L. (1996). Effects of blood alcohol concentrations on negative punishment: Implications for decision making. *Journal of Studies on Alcohol, 57,* 85-94.

National Highway Traffic Safety Administration. (1996). *Traffic Safety Facts 1995: A Compilation of Motor Vehicle Crash Data from the Fatal Accident Reporting System and the General Estimates System* (DOT HS 808 471). Washington, DC: U.S. Government Printing Office.

Shore, E.R., Gregory, T., & Tatlock, L. (1991). College students' reactions to a designated driver program: An exploratory study. *Journal of Alcohol and Drug Education, 37,* 1-6.

Voas, R. B. (1997). Drinking and driving prevention in the community: Program planning and implementation. *Addiction, (Supplement 2).*

Wagenaar, A.C. (1992). Designated driver programs: A commentary on the DeJong and Wallack Article. *Health Education Quarterly, 19,* 443-445.

Winstein, J.A. (1994). Promoting designated drivers: The Harvard alcohol project. *American Journal of Preventive Medicine, 10,* 11-14.

Targeting DWI Prevention

William F. Wieczorek

Buffalo State College

James J. Coyle

Research Institute on Addictions

SUMMARY. This project studied the variation in the rate of DWI in small communities as represented by census tracts. The study examined the communities where the DWI offenders reside, not where they were arrested. The concept is that DWI prevention can be targeted at communities with high rates of DWI. The home address of every person who was convicted of a drinking and driving offense from 1990-1994 and resided in Erie County was geocoded (n = 15,551). This provided a geographic reference that allowed all of the offenders to be aggregated into the appropriate census tract. The results showed that on-premise alcohol outlets were significantly related to the DWI rate. In addition, higher proportions of males, non-skilled occupations, and whites were related significantly to higher DWI rates. The findings strongly indicate that there is a spatial pattern of DWI offenders in communities. The specific characteristics of these high DWI communities can be used to more effectively target places and populations for DWI prevention programs. *[Article copies available for a fee from The Haworth Document Delivery Service: 1-800-342-9678. E-mail address: getinfo@haworth.com]*

This research was supported by National Institutes of Health grants R01AA10305 and K02AA00154.

[Haworth co-indexing entry note]: "Targeting DWI Prevention." Wieczorek, William F., and James J. Coyle. Co-published simultaneously in *Journal of Prevention & Intervention in the Community* (The Haworth Press, Inc.) Vol. 17, No. 1, 1998, pp. 15-30; and: *Preventing Drunk Driving* (ed: Elsie R. Shore, and Joseph R. Ferrari) The Haworth Press, Inc., 1998, pp. 15-30. Single or multiple copies of this article are available for a fee from The Haworth Document Delivery Service [1-800-342-9678, 9:00 a.m. - 5:00 p.m. (EST). E-mail address: getinfo@haworth.com].

INTRODUCTION

Driving while impaired or intoxicated (DWI) by alcohol continues to present enormous public health, criminal justice, and traffic safety problems. Over 40% of crash fatalities are alcohol related, which amounts to about 17,000 alcohol-related fatalities each year (United States Department of Transportation [USDOT], 1995). Alcohol is involved in an additional estimated 180,000 to 1.2 million crashes with property damage, and 200,000-300,000 personal injury crashes every year (USDOT, 1984; USDOT, 1989). DWI is the most common offense category in the United States, with an estimated 1.52 million arrests in 1993 (Maguire & Pastore, 1995, p. 374). Clearly, the negative social, economic, and health consequences of DWI provide strong justification for efforts to reduce its impact.

A review of the DWI literature shows that a broad spectrum of prevention approaches have been suggested and implemented (c.f. Saltz et al., 1995; U.S. Department of Health and Human Services, 1989). DWI prevention efforts to date have focused mainly on factors associated with the individual and the drinking context. Some of the DWI prevention efforts focused at individuals are mass media campaigns (Atkin, 1989; Simons-Morton & Simons-Morton, 1989; Vingilis & Coltes, 1990), programs to change DWI-related norms (Barokas, 1995), and warning labels on alcoholic beverages (Saltz et al., 1995). Police and the criminal justice system utilize enforcement efforts and sanctions to deter individuals from DWI (Ross, 1992; Wieczorek, Mirand, & Callahan, 1994). In addition, treatment for alcohol problems can produce secondary prevention effects on DWI offenders (Wieczorek, 1995).

The drinking context, including the alcohol beverage distribution system, has been the focus of a number of possible interventions for reducing DWI (Wagenaar & Farrell, 1989). A reduction in alcohol availability through a decrease in the density of outlets is a form of DWI prevention because a number of studies have found a relationship between alcohol availability, particularly the density of on-premise alcohol outlets, and DWI (Gruenewald et al., 1996; Mann & Anglin, 1990; Scribner, MacKinnon, & Dwyer, 1994). Other methods of DWI prevention through reduced alcohol access are increases in the minimum age to purchase alcohol (O'Malley & Wagenaar, 1991; Wagenaar, 1983), and raising the cost of alcohol through taxes (Cook, 1981). DWI prevention programs targeted at the drinking context, rather than availability, include training for persons who serve alcohol (Saltz, 1989; Holder & Wagenaar, 1994), and safe ride or designated driver programs (Apsler, 1989).

Geographic Targeting of DWI Prevention

The DWI prevention efforts mentioned above reflect a wide variety of approaches, some which have specific targets of influence (e.g., beverage servers), and others which have extremely broad purposes (e.g., alcohol availability and taxes). There is no specific intent to target DWI prevention activities toward areas where DWI is especially common, although specific DWI prevention activities (e.g., interventions implemented at outlets, sobriety checkpoints for enforcement) have an implicit geographic component. To date, the issue of targeting DWI prevention efforts at specific communities within a larger geographic framework has not been examined. DWI is amenable to targeting and community-level analysis because the high frequency of DWI provides sufficient numbers to be aggregated even in small areas.

To determine whether there is a spatial pattern of DWI that could be used to target prevention to higher risk communities, this study examined the DWI offense rate for small areas defined by census tracts within Erie County, New York. Census tracts are areas that have a population of approximately 4,000 persons, and are one of the basic geographic units used to report population information for communities in the United States. To investigate factors associated with the variation in DWI, alcohol availability information and sociodemographic variables were utilized in bivariate correlation and multiple regression analysis. Alcohol availability and sociodemographic characteristics such as males, whites, unskilled occupations, lower education, lower income, and younger age have been associated with DWI and related problems (Perrine, Peck, & Fell, 1989; Mann & Anglin, 1990, Scribner et al., 1994).

The study focuses on the home address of the DWI offenders, not the location where that offense occurred, because the home address identifies communities where DWI behaviors are most common.

This facilitates a community-based approach to DWI prevention that utilizes small communities, as defined by census tracts.

METHOD

This study was conducted in Erie County, NY. Erie County has a population of about 968,000, and includes a large core city (Buffalo), and suburban and semi-rural areas. Erie County is divided into 236 census tracts, of which nine were not included in the study because the majority of the population in these tracts were institutional (e.g., hospitals, prisons), or were missing the majority of the census data (e.g., Indian reservations). The DWI offender data were provided by the New York State Department of Motor Vehicles for the years 1990 to 1994. Drivers convicted of any drinking and driving offense were included in the study. The data provided only the home address of the DWI offenders. There were 15,551 DWI offenders in the data set. The home address was geocoded (i.e., provided a digital spatial reference by matching the address with geographic coordinates) so that each offender could be aggregated to a census tract. To accomplish the geocoding, the Census Bureau's topologically integrated geographic encoding and referencing (TIGER) system was used to create street-level maps for address matching, and digital boundaries for tracts in Erie County (Marx, 1990; Bureau of the Census, 1990). In addition, a database of all tax parcels of land, including geographic coordinates, was used to assist the geocoding process. After geocoding, DWI offenders were aggregated into the appropriate census tract. A DWI rate was calculated for each tract by dividing the number of DWI offenders by the tract population, and expressing the result as DWIs per 10,000 persons.

Alcohol availability was based on 1994 alcohol license data provided by the State Liquor Authority. Alcohol outlets were categorized as on-premise outlets (alcohol is purchased and consumed on site; $n = 1,422$), and off-premise outlets (alcohol is purchased for consumption elsewhere; $n = 1,017$). Using the same method as for the DWI offenders, alcohol outlets were geocoded, allocated to census tracts, and converted to a rate per 10,000 persons separately for on- and off-premise types.

The sociodemographic information for Erie County was obtained from census tract data from the STF-3A CD-ROM (Bureau of the Census, 1992). The measures derived from this source were median family income, percent male, percent not high school graduates, percent in unskilled occupations, percent aged 18 to 39 years, and a dummy coded race variable. The race variable was dummy coded as 1 = majority white, 0 = majority non-white, because the distribution of the variable was bimodal with large numbers of tracts consisting of a high percentage of white or minority population.

Analytic Approach

The study examined the bivariate Pearson correlations and multivariate associations of DWI with alcohol availability, spatial, and sociodemographic variables. The spatial variable was the generalized spatial potential, based on the geographic distribution of the DWI variable. A generalized spatial potential (GSP) variable was calculated to determine if the geographic distribution of DWI showed spatial autocorrelation. Spatial autocorrelation exists when location or proximity to other tracts is a significant predictor of an areal variable, such as DWI rate (Duncan et al., 1963; Roncek & Montgomery, 1994). Autocorrelation indicates that the spatial distribution of the variable is not random. The generalized spatial potential in this study utilized the DWI rate and distance to other tracts. The GSP can be conceptualized as a type of a gravity model, where places with high values for DWI rate are likely to be closer to other areas with higher DWI rates (Ricketts et al., 1994).

The generalized spatial potential was calculated for each tract as $GSP_i = V_1/D_1 + V_2/D_2 + \ldots V_n/D_n$, where V is the value of the dependent variable (DWI rate) in a tract, D is the distance from tract i to the other tract, and n is the number of tracts, not including tract i. The GSP as used in this study offered a simple technique to examine whether there was spatial autocorrelation, and to account for this effect in the regression. However, substantially more effort would be needed to refine the potential and calculate potentials for additional variables, if the main purpose of the study was a spatial model to predict DWI.

The multiple regression utilized ordinary least squares technique and a hierarchical approach. In the multiple regression, the generalized spatial potential was forced into the equation at the first step, followed by a stepwise selection of the remaining predictors using a significance level of p ≤ .05. The spatial autocorrelation in DWI rate was controlled by forcing the GSP into the equation at the first step.

RESULTS

Figure 1 is a map showing the variation of DWI rate based on quintiles, which are five categories each consisting of an equal number of census tracts. The mean DWI rate for census tracts in Erie County was 160 per 10,000 (± 72 per 10,000) persons. Urban areas are reflected by the small physical size of the tracts, and rural areas are characterized by large area tracts. The map clearly indicates that there were notable geographic differences in the DWI rate. Figure 1 shows that high DWI rate tracts were found in urban, suburban, and rural areas. Also note that there was a recognizable group of lower DWI rate tracts in the urban core of the city of Buffalo. The map of DWI rates by tract strongly suggests that DWI offenders were not randomly distributed, and supports the concept that DWI prevention resources could be targeted.

The results of the correlation analysis are shown in Table 1. All of the variables, except off-premise availability and median family income, were significantly correlated with the DWI rate. The moderately strong, positive correlation between the generalized spatial potential and DWI rate indicated that there was a spatial pattern of tracts having a similar DWI rate to nearby tracts. On-premise availability was directly correlated with the DWI rate, suggesting that drinking establishments tend to increase DWIs. Variables measuring majority white population, percent unskilled jobs, and percent not high school graduates were all directly associated with the DWI rate. The proportion of persons aged 18 to 39 was weakly, inversely associated with the DWI rate in these data.

An examination of Table 1 shows that three variables in addition to the DWI rate were significantly correlated with the GSP. This finding suggests that these variables have a significantly similar spatial distribution as the DWI rate. Measures of on-premise avail-

FIGURE 1. Erie County DWI rate by census tract

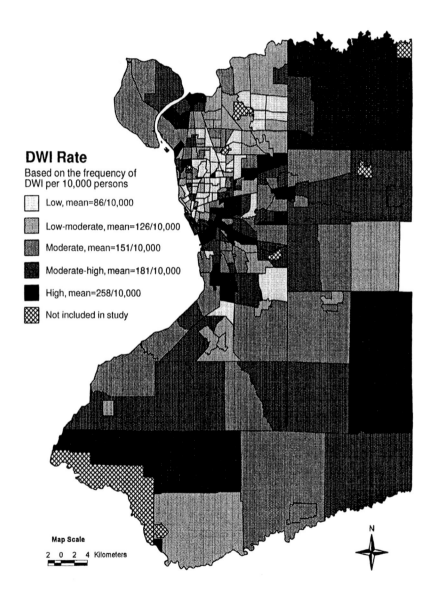

DWI Rate

Based on the frequency of
DWI per 10,000 persons

Low, mean=86/10,000

Low-moderate, mean=126/10,000

Moderate, mean=151/10,000

Moderate-high, mean=181/10,000

High, mean=258/10,000

Not included in study

Map Scale

2 0 2 4 Kilometers

N

TABLE 1. Bivariate correlations between DWI rate, alcohol availability, and demographic variables

Variables	1	2	3	4	5	6	7	8	9
(1) DWIRate	--								
(2) Generalized Potential	.59***	--							
(3) Off-premise outlets	-0.13	0.02	--						
(4) On-premise outlets	.29***	.26***	.36***	--					
(5) Males (%)	.22***	0.04	0.12	.34**	--				
(6) Persons 18-39(%)	-0.17**	0.11	0.10	-0.10	0.05	--			
(7) Not H.S. grads (%)	.15**	.43***	.50***	.34***	.03**	-0.09	--		
(8) Non-skilled jobs (%)	.33***	0.31	.33***	.28***	0.09	0.05	.73***	--	
(9) Race (1= majority white)	.32***	0.01	-.44***	0.02	-0.04	-0.03	-.48***	-.37***	--
(10) Median family income	-0.12	-.44***	-.37***	-.29***	0.05	-0.17**	-.84***	-.75***	.48***

Note: (n = 227)
*p ≤ .05
**p ≤ .01
***p ≤ .001

ability and percent not high school graduates were directly associated with the GSP. Note that while on-premise availability was significantly associated with the GSP, off-premise availability was not associated with the GSP. Median family income was inversely related to the GSP, suggesting that the spatial pattern of DWI is associated with lower incomes.

On-premise and off-premise alcohol availability had a direct and significant correlation. Although off-premise availability was not significantly associated with the DWI rate, both off-premise and on-premise availability had a similar pattern of correlations indicating that availability was associated with less education, unskilled jobs, and lower income. There were two differences in the correlation patterns of off- and on-premise availability. Off-premise availability was significantly associated with race, indicating that off-premise availability tended to be higher in areas where the majority of the population was not white. On-premise availability was correlated with sex, indicating that on-premise availability was higher in tracts with more men.

Table 1 also shows a number of noteworthy intercorrelations among the sociodemographic variables. Lower educational attainment (percent not high school graduates) was associated with lower income, unskilled occupations, and tracts where the majority of the population is not white. Similarly, unskilled occupations and percent persons 18 to 39 years of age were significantly associated with lower median incomes. Finally, both unskilled jobs and lower median incomes were associated with tracts where the majority of the population is not white.

A multivariate analytic approach was used to facilitate a more sophisticated evaluation of the factors associated with DWI by examining the simultaneous influence of the predictors. A hierarchical, stepwise multiple regression analysis was performed with DWI as the dependent variable. The generalized spatial potential was forced into the multiple regression at the first step. The remaining predictors were then entered by using a stepwise selection with a significance level of $p \leq .05$. The results of the multiple regression analysis are shown in Table 2. Similar to the bivariate analysis, the GSP was significantly and positively associated with DWI. GSP had the largest beta in the final equation, which signifies that it was the most influential predictor. Although each of the steps is not shown in Table 2, the addition of the GSP at the first step attenuated the beta coefficients for all of the other predictors not in the equation. However, none of the predictors became nonsignificant, indicating that the spatial effect accounted for by the GSP does not account for all of the statistically significant relationship between DWI and sociodemographic variables.

The results of the multiple regression tended to coincide with the bivariate findings. On-premise availability was the only variable

TABLE 2. Multiple regression analysis of DWI rate on spatial, alcohol, and demographic variables

Predictors of DWI Rate	Beta	T
Generalized spatial potential	.60	13.58***
Persons 18-39 (%)	−.30	−7.53***
Males (%)	.17	4.31***
Not H.S. grads (%)	−.35	−5.28***
Non-skilled jobs (%)	.53	9.28***
Race (1 = majority white)	.34	7.66***

***$p < .0001$

that was significant in bivariate correlation, but not significant in the multiple regression. The proportion of unskilled jobs in each tract was the second most influential variable in the final regression equation. The sign of the beta corresponds with the bivariate analysis, which indicated that tracts higher in unskilled occupations were associated with higher DWI rates. The percent of the population aged 18 to 39 was negatively associated with DWI in the multiple regression. The multiple regression also found that tracts with majority white population and a higher percent of males were directly related to the DWI rate.

One major difference between the bivariate analysis and the multiple regression was the finding for educational attainment. The percent not having at least a high school education in each tract was positively correlated with DWI in the bivariate analysis. In the multiple regression, however, this measure of tract-level educational attainment was negatively associated with DWI. This reversal in the valence of the sign from positive in correlation to negative in the multiple regression identified the education measure (percent not attaining at least a high school diploma) as a suppressor variable (Tabachnik & Fidel, 1983), and clearly illustrates the advantage of simultaneously examining the relationships between the independent variables and the dependent variable. Thus, when variables such as the GSP, occupation, and race were controlled for in the regression, the percent who did not graduate from high school was inversely related to DWI.

DISCUSSION

Efforts to target DWI prevention to specific geographic areas or communities where DWI is particularly common is virtually unknown, with the possible exception of sobriety checkpoints. Sobriety checkpoints, however, are targeted at roads rather than the communities where the DWI offenders reside. In comparison, the mental health field, including substance abuse, has developed models of the need for services based on estimates of mental health problems in small areas (Ciarlo & Tweed, 1992). Most of the mental health services models have been used to estimate need for treatment, rather than prevention, although the relevance of the small area approach for targeting prevention services also has been recognized (Breer, McAuliffe, & Levine, 1996; Wieczorek & Coyle, 1996).

The results of the present study provide strong support for the concept of targeting DWI prevention efforts at localities with higher DWI rates. The map of DWI for Erie County provided strong visual evidence of substantial variation in DWI across small areas. The correlation analysis found DWI to have significant spatial autocorrelation, which indicated that tracts tend to be located near other tracts with similar DWI rates. The spatial effect also was significant in the multivariate regression analysis, as were other predictors of DWI such as gender, race, occupation, age structure, and education. These findings are especially relevant because the predictors provide substantial insight regarding the composition of the population in tracts with high DWI rates.

The findings from the correlation and multiple regression analyses tended to correspond with the literature on DWI offenders (Perrine, Peck, & Fell, 1989). DWI rates were higher in areas with more males, unskilled occupations, majority white populations, and greater on-premise alcohol availability, which coincides with the DWI literature. Two results may be a product of the unique education and age structure of the study area. First, the relationship of DWI with the percent of the population between ages 18 to 39 was inverse instead of direct. The most likely explanation of this finding is that the tracts with the youngest populations (high percent 18 to 39) were located in highly urbanized areas where DWI was low. Second, the multivariate analysis found that low educational attainment, measured as percent without a high school education, was associated with tracts having lower DWI rates. This finding also could be explained by lower educational attainment being more common in the highly urban tracts.

Although DWI exists to some extent in almost all communities, the evidence indicated that DWI was not evenly distributed in the population or geographically. The results provided substantial insight regarding alcohol availability and population characteristics of places where DWI rates were higher. The results of this study indicated that a higher level of on-premise alcohol availability, higher percent male population, majority white population, and unskilled occupations, were community-level characteristics associated with higher DWI rates. Prevention planners can use these population characteristics to develop interventions tailored to the interests and lifestyle of high DWI areas. For example, DWI prevention could be developed for specific apartment complexes as a target within a tract where DWI is high because the residents are likely to have characteristics similar to the DWI population.

Moreover, the findings from this study identify geographic locations where DWI prevention should be targeted. Of course all areas where any drinkers and any drivers reside may require some DWI prevention; however, focusing specific prevention efforts at places with particularly high rates of DWI offers a method for optimizing the impact of prevention. A spectrum of DWI prevention approaches, as mentioned in the introduction, could be directed toward specific high DWI locations. On-premise alcohol outlets located within high DWI communities would be excellent sites to focus DWI prevention efforts. The bivariate analysis showed a relationship between on-premise alcohol availability and DWI rate, which suggests that DWI offenders tend to drink at nearby on-premise locations. Server intervention training, safe ride programs, and new programs that target DWI norms could be implemented at on-premise establishments. Safe ride programs such as designated drivers, ride sharing, and organized safe ride programs where a taxi or other service provides transportation could be developed. General alcohol control polices offer additional approaches to reduce DWI (Saltz et al., 1995). Furthermore, these interventions could be directed differentially toward tracts with high DWI rates.

Sobriety checkpoints should be focused on tracts where DWI is common. Community mobilization by anti-DWI citizen organizations, such as Mothers Against Drunk Driving (MADD) and Remove Intoxicated Drivers (RID), can be disproportionately directed at specific high DWI communities. Students Against Drunk Driving (SADD) chapters could be encouraged to develop at schools in high DWI communities. The content of school-based substance abuse prevention programs could increase the amount of material that focuses on DWI and associated issues such as riding with impaired drivers. DWI offenders are known to have high rates of substance abuse problems, which would make high DWI areas prime locations for finding cases for treatment. Treatment has been shown to offer substantial benefit for reducing DWI recidivism and fatalities (Well-Parker et al., 1995, Wieczorek, 1995).

There are some additional considerations regarding the targeting of prevention for DWI. Geographic targeting of DWI prevention may not be possible in places where the DWI conviction rate is low because the number of convictions may be insufficient to provide stable estimates in small geographic areas, and the pattern of convictions may be biased and provide a misleading spatial pattern of DWI. For similar reasons, DWI targeting may be most appropriate in areas with populations large enough to be divided into more than a few census tracts. Furthermore, the use of DWI rate data for the targeting of general substance abuse prevention services should be used with caution. Some minorities, such as African Americans, tend to be under-represented in DWI arrest statistics (Breer et al., 1996). Additional indicators that adequately cover the prevention needs of African Americans should be used to supplement DWI data in multivariate models appropriate for targeting general substance abuse prevention services.

The results of this study provide strong evidence that the targeting of DWI prevention is highly feasible. The development and coordination of a targeted DWI prevention campaign is a challenging task. Future research will need to determine whether targeted prevention programs can be implemented, and whether these programs result in a corresponding decrease in DWI and related behaviors.

REFERENCES

Apsler, R. (1989). Transportation alternatives for drinkers. In *Surgeon General's Workshop on Drunk Driving Background Papers* (pp. 157-168). Washington, DC: U.S. Department of Health and Human Services.

Atkin, C.K. (1989). Mass communication effects on drinking and driving. In *Surgeon General's Workshop on Drunk Driving Background Papers* (pp. 15-34). Washington, DC: U.S. Department of Health and Human Services.

Barokas, J. (1995). *Lessons learned from public health campaigns and applied to anti-DWI norms development.* Washington, DC: U.S. Department of Transportation National Highway Traffic Safety Administration.

Breer, P., McAuliffe, W.E., & Levine, E.B. (1996). Statewide substance abuse prevention planning. *Evaluation Review, 20*(5), 596-618.

Bureau of the Census (1990). *TIGER: The coast-to-coast digital map data base.* U.S. Department of Commerce.

Bureau of the Census (1992). *Census of population and housing, 1990: Summary tape file 3 on CD-ROM technical documentation.*

Ciaro, J.A., & Tweed D.L. (1992). VI. Implementing indirect needs-assessment models for planning state mental health and substance abuse services. *Evaluation and Program Planning, 15,* 195-210.

Cook, P.J. (1981). The effect of liquor taxes on drinking, cirrhosis and auto accidents, In M.H. Moore and D.R. Gerstein (Eds.), *Alcohol and public policy: Beyond the shadow of prohibition* (pp. 255-285). Washington, DC: National Academy Press.

Duncan, O.D., Cuzzort, R.P., & Duncan, B.A. (1963). *Statistical Geography.* New York: Free Press.

Gruenewald, P.J., Millar, A.B., Treno, A.J., Yang, Z., Ponicki, W.R., & Roeper, P. (1996). The geography of availability and driving after drinking. *Addiction, 91,* 967-983.

Holder, H.D., & Wagenaar, A.C. (1994). Mandated server training and reduced alcohol-involved traffic crashes: A time series analysis of the Oregon experience. *Accident Anal Prev 26*(1), 89-97.

Maguire, K., & Pastore, A.L. (1995). *Bureau of Justice Statistics Sourcebook of Criminal Justice Statistics–1994.* (NCJ-154591). Washington, D.C.: U.S. Department of Justice.

Mann, R.E., & Anglin, L. (1990). Alcohol availability, per capita consumption, and the alcohol-crash problem. In R.J. Wilson & R.E. Mann (Eds.), *Drinking and driving: Advances in research and prevention* (pp. 205-225). New York: The Guilford Press.

Marx, R.W. (1990). The TIGER system: Yesterday, today and tomorrow. *Cartography and Geographic Information Systems 17,* 89-97.

O'Malley, P.M., & Wagenaar, A.C. (1991). Effects of minimum drinking age laws on alcohol use, related behaviors and traffic crash involvement among American youth. *Journal of Studies on Alcohol, 52,* 478-491.

Perrine, M.W., Peck, R.C., & Fell, J.C. (1989). Epidemiologic perspectives on drunken driving, In *Surgeon General's Workshop on Drunk Driving Back-*

ground Papers (pp. 36-76). Rockville, MD: U.S. Department of Health and Human Services.

Ricketts, T.C., Savitz, L.A., Gesler, W.M., & Osborne, D.N. (1994). *Geographic methods for health services research.* Lanham, MD: University Press of America.

Roncek, D.W., & Montgomery, A. (1994). Spatial autocorrelation revisited: Conceptual underpinnings and practical guidelines for the use of the generalized potential as a remedy for spatial autocorrelation in large samples. In *Workshop on crime analysis through computer mapping proceedings: 1993.* (pp. 141-155). Chicago: Illinois Criminal Justice Information Authority.

Ross, H.L. (1992). *Confronting drunk driving: Social policies for saving lives.* New Haven, CT: Yale University Press.

Saltz, R.F. (1989). Server intervention and responsible beverage service programs. In *Surgeon General's Workshop on Drunk Driving Background Papers* (pp. 169-191). Washington, DC: U.S. Department of Health and Human Services.

Saltz, R.F., Holder, H.D., Grube, J.W., Gruenewald, P.J., & Voas, R.B. (1995). Prevention strategies for reducing alcohol problems including alcohol-related trauma. In R.R. Watson (Ed.), *Alcohol, cocaine and accidents* (pp. 57-83). Totowa, NJ: Humana Press.

Scribner, R.A., MacKinnon, D.P., & Dwyer, J.H. (1994). Alcohol outlet density and motor vehicle crashes in Los Angeles County cities. *Journal of Studies on Alcohol, 55,* 447-453

Simons-Morton, B.G., & Simons-Morton, D.G. (1989). Controlling injuries due to drinking and driving: The context and functions of education. In *Surgeon General's Workshop on Driving Background Papers* (pp. 77-92). Washington, DC: U.S. Department of Health and Human Services.

Tabachnik, B.G., & Fidel, L.S. (1983). *Using multivariate statistics.* New York: Harper & Row.

U.S. Department of Health and Human Services. (1989). *Surgeon General's Workshop on Drunk Driving Background Papers.* Washington, DC: U.S. Department of Health and Human Services.

U.S. Department of Transportation. (1984). *Alcohol and highway safety 1984: A review of the state of the knowledge.* Washington, DC: National Highway Traffic Safety Administration.

U.S. Department of Transportation (1989). *Alcohol and highway safety 1989: A review of the state of the knowledge.* Washington, DC: National Highway Traffic Safety Administration.

U.S. Department of Transportation (1995). *Traffic Safety Facts, 1994.* National Highway Traffic Safety Administration, Washington, DC.

Vingilis, E., & Coltes, B. (1990). Mass communications and drinking-driving: Theories, practices and results. *Alcohol, Drugs, Driving 6*(2), 61-81.

Wagenaar, A.C. (1983). *Alcohol, young drivers and traffic accidents.* Lexington, MA: Lexington Books.

Wagenaar, A.C., & Farrell, S. (1989). Alcohol beverage control policies: Their role in preventing alcohol-impaired driving. In *Surgeon General's Workshop on Drunk Driving Background Papers* (pp. 1-14). Washington, DC: U.S. Department of Health and Human Services.

Wells-Parker, E., Bangert-Drowns, R., McMillen, R., & Williams, M. (1995). Final results from a meta-analysis of remedial interventions with drink/drive offenders. *Addiction, 90,* 907-926.

Wieczorek, W.F. (1995). The role of treatment in reducing alcohol-related accidents involving DWI offenders. In Watson, R.R. (Ed.), *Alcohol, cocaine, and accidents* (pp. 105-129), Totowa, NJ:Humana Press.

Wieczorek, W.F., & Coyle, J.J. (1996). Categorical models of the need for alcohol-related services in small areas. *Alcoholism: Clinical and Experimental Research, 20*(2) Supplement, 145A.

Wieczorek, W.F., Mirand, A.L., & Callahan, C.P. (1994). Perception of the risk of arrest for drinking-and-driving. *Criminal Justice and Behavior, 21,* 312-324.

Vehicle Interlock Programs: Protecting the Community Against the Drunk Driver

Paul R. Marques
Robert B. Voas

The Pacific Institute for Research and Evaluation

David Hodgins

Addictions Centre

SUMMARY. People convicted of drunk-driving offenses have an 80% higher likelihood of being involved in fatal crashes. License suspension is an effective but incomplete sanction as many offenders continue to drive unlicensed. Breath alcohol ignition interlock devices, which require a low alcohol breath sample before a car will start, hold promise for the control of some drunk driving offenders. Evidence shows these devices are effective while installed on the cars of those who elect to install them, but that elective use is still low, and even if installed recidivism rates climb once the interlock period is completed. This paper reviews interlock program problem areas and presents a plan for a brief intervention/case management program which is currently being tested in Alberta, Canada. *[Article copies available for a fee from The Haworth Document Delivery Service: 1-800-342-9678. E-mail address: getinfo@haworth.com]*

This work was supported by NIAAA grant No. RO1 AA10320.

[Haworth co-indexing entry note]: "Vehicle Interlock Programs: Protecting the Community Against the Drunk Driver." Marques, Paul R., Robert B. Voas, and David Hodgins. Co-published simultaneously in *Journal of Prevention & Intervention in the Community* (The Haworth Press, Inc.) Vol. 17, No. 1, 1998, pp. 31-44; and: *Preventing Drunk Driving* (ed: Elsie R. Shore, and Joseph R. Ferrari) The Haworth Press, Inc., 1998, pp. 31-44. Single or multiple copies of this article are available for a fee from The Haworth Document Delivery Service [1-800-342-9678, 9:00 a.m. - 5:00 p.m. (EST). E-mail address: getinfo@haworth.com].

INTRODUCTION

Few events are more tragic than the death of an innocent road user caused by an impaired driver, especially one who continues to drive illegally despite having a suspended license from a prior drunken-driving conviction. Drivers with driving-under-the-influence (DUI) offenses are 1.8 times as likely to be involved in a fatal crash of any kind, and 4.1 times as likely to be intoxicated at the time of an accident (Hedlund and Fell, 1992). The odds of involvement in an alcohol-related fatal crash for those with two or more DUI convictions is 36 times higher than that of drivers without such convictions (Brewer et al., 1994). Efforts to control the recidivism of DUI offenders can be classified under four headings: *deterrence, treatment, supervision, and incapacitation.* The alcohol interlock is the newest form of incapacitation. This paper reviews past control strategies and introduces worthwhile features of an alcohol interlock program.

Deterrence. Historically, the use of severe penalties, including fines and jail, has been the preferred method for controlling drunken drivers. However, jail has proven to be of limited effectiveness as a specific deterrent for DUI offenders (Nichols and Ross, 1988; Simpson, Mayhew, and Beirness, 1996). A recent evaluation of electronic home confinement by Jones et al. (1996) suggests that this alternative mode of incarceration may have some value in reducing DUI recidivism, although it has not yet received systematic study for alcohol offenders.

Treatment. The apparent failure of traditional punitive sanctions to deter repeat offenders led to the acknowledgment of the role of alcohol dependence and addiction in the drinking-driving problem and then to development of special education and treatment programs for DUI offenders (Stewart and Melfetti, 1970; Nichols, Weinstein, and Ellingstad, 1980). Initial studies of these programs suggested that they were not as effective in reducing crash involvement as long-term license suspension (Hagen, 1978; Sadler and Perrine, 1984). This appeared to be due to the fact that a promised reduction in the period of license revocation was used to motivate the offenders to attend treatment. However, later studies in which the period of license suspension was controlled showed that treatment programs did reduce alcohol-related crashes and DUI recidivism rates beyond the effect of license suspension alone (McKnight and Voas, 1991). An extensive meta-analysis of 215 independent evaluations of education and treatment programs found an average reduction of 8% to 9% in both DUI recidivism and alcohol-related crashes, whereas licensing sanctions alone "tended to be associated with the reduction of non-alcohol crashes" (Wells-Parker, Banger-et-Drowns, McMillen and Williams, 1995).

Supervision. An intervention that has received less study than treatment programs is the use of supervision to reduce recidivism. California implemented a law providing for the treatment of multiple DUI offenders combined with brief (15-minute) biweekly interviews with a probation officer. An evaluation of that program by Reis (1982) indicated that the 15-minute biweekly interviews had approximately the same impact on recidivism as a 6 month, weekly group therapy program. Voas and Tippetts (1990) found that a short interview held weekly for a year with first offenders was as effective as a 28-day residential treatment program. Jones et al. (1996) evaluated an intensive probation monitoring program for multiple offenders in Milwaukee and found that it reduced recidivism to 8.5% compared to 16% for the comparison group.

Incapacitation Through License Suspension. The most effective long-term method for reducing overall accident involvement of DUI offenders has been incapacitation through license suspension (Nichols and Ross 1988). However, the ability of license suspension to control impaired driving is limited by the ease with which suspended operators can continue to drive with little fear of apprehension. The difficulty in supervising this driving prohibition through enforcement of the license suspension penalty results in up to 75% of suspended DUIs continuing to drive (Nichols and Ross, 1988). As a result, eleven percent of the drivers involved in fatal crashes are unlicensed (Hedlund and Fell, 1995). Moreover, the ease of driving while suspended results in approximately half of the DUI offenders not bothering to reapply for license reinstatement when eligible (Voas and McKnight, 1989; Sadler and Perrine, 1984). Voas, Tippetts and Lange (1997) found that in Oregon, where the suspension period for a first DUI is 3 months, half of the offenders were still suspended 5 years after their conviction date.

Incapacitation Through Vehicle Sanctions. Because of the limited effectiveness of license suspension in fully incapacitating the high-risk DUI offender, legislative attention has recently been drawn to action against the offender's vehicle. Evaluation of the Oregon "Zebra Sticker" program (Voas, Tippetts, and Lange, 1997) has provided evidence that marking the license plates of vehicles driven by unlicensed drivers can reduce DWS (driving while suspended) and DUI offenses. In Minnesota, an administrative revocation of the vehicle registration and the seizing of the vehicle plates for third-time DUI offenders has been shown to reduce subsequent recidivism (Rogers, 1994). Voas, Tippetts and Taylor (1997) have shown that a law providing for the impoundment and immobilization of vehicles of multiple DUI offenders for up to 6 months in Ohio produced a reduction in recidivism, not only during the time the vehicle was impounded or immobilized, but also during the period following its return to the offender.

VEHICLE INTERLOCKS

A popular alternative to depriving the offender (and the offender's family) of the use of his or her vehicle is the installation of an alcohol safety interlock device that prevents the vehicle from starting when an operator has a BAC above .02 to .03. This device, initially proposed by Voas (1970), has only recently has been enhanced with adequate behavioral monitoring systems and procedures to prevent circumvention. Since issuance of performance guidelines drafted by Voas and Marques for NHTSA (National Highway Traffic Safety Administration), and a companion document describing state-level monitoring programs (Voas and Marques, 1992). The use of interlocks has spread rapidly. As of January 1997, 34 states had enacted legislation providing for interlock programs. The NHTSA guidelines, in addition to specifying the sensitivity of the devices to alcohol and the procedures for preventing circumvention, also established a requirement for retesting while driving and a data logger system to record every breath test taken by a motorist on all trips in the instrumented vehicle. This is intended to detect efforts to circumvent the interlock.

Evaluations of Interlock Programs. There has been only one random trial of an interlock program (Beck, Rauch, and Baker, unpublished). Only the first year's results are available for this in-progress Maryland study. The study involves two remedial programs for multiple DUI offenders seeking to have their operator permits reinstated. One program to which 698 offenders were assigned, provided for installation of the interlock along with attendance at Alcoholics Anonymous (AA) meetings. While only 56.7% of this group actually installed interlocks on their vehicles, the group's one year recidivism rate was 2.4% compared to 6.7% for the 689 members of the comparison group who were placed on a drunk-driving treatment and monitoring program in lieu of requiring the interlock. This result is in line with earlier demonstrations of the effectiveness of interlock programs that did not involve random assignment.

Elliott and Morse (1993) reported on a study of the recidivism of convicted drunk drivers paired for the interlock and full suspension. During the first 12 months following conviction, the drivers with interlocks on their vehicles had a significantly lower recidivism rate (2.9% vs. 8.4%). But, in the following 12 months, when the driving privileges of both groups had been restored, the recidivism rates were essentially identical (6.6% vs. 6.4%). Popkin et al. (1993) in North Carolina, Jones (1992) in Oregon and Tippetts and Voas (1997) in West Virginia all obtained similar results–evidence of sizeable reductions in recidivism while the interlock device is installed on the vehicle but with no differences in recidivism rates with comparison offenders after the interlock is removed. The one exception to this pattern of results is the study reported by Weinrath (1997) in Alberta, Canada, where he also found a significant reduction in recidivism during interlock installation, but in addition found a small, but significant, reduction in recidivism during a 15-month period following the removal of the unit.

Interlock Limitations. A significant limitation on all the evaluations of interlock programs to date is the relatively few offenders who agree to have a unit installed on their vehicles. Simpson, Mayhew, and Beirness (1996) reported that in their survey of interlock programs, only 5% of first offenders and 2% of second offenders in Michigan, 2% and 1% of first and second offenders in Nebraska, and 4% of all DUI offenders in Wisconsin were in interlock programs. Tippetts and Voas (1997) found that fewer than 3% of DUI offenders in West Virginia were in the state's interlock program. This low participation in interlock programs limits their effectiveness. The reasons for low participation have received little attention. While some offenders do not drive while suspended, for those offenders who intend to keep driving, the choice is between installing the interlock or driving while suspended. It appears that the cost and annoyance of the interlock–a breath sample must be provided periodically while driving–outweighs the risk of being apprehended for driving while suspended. The fact that half of DUI offenders do not apply for reinstatement of their driver's license when eligible to do so is evidence that fear of driving while suspended is a weak incentive to motivate acceptance of the interlock.

Summary. It appears that current hardware design features block most efforts to bypass or circumvent the interlock. However, there are three significant limitations to the effectiveness of interlock programs: (1) only a small proportion of DUI offenders agree to accept the interlock on their vehicles; (2) interlock users, like most drivers, have access to vehicles without interlocks; and (3) the improved safety behavior forced by the program appears not to continue after the interlock is removed. Despite these limitations, the accumulating evidence that the interlock protects the public by reducing DUI recidivism, and the concern that traditional unsupervised license suspension is losing its effectiveness, is likely to lead to increased use of this sanction.

DEVELOPMENT OF AN INTERLOCK SUPPORT PROGRAM

To deal with the limitations in current interlock programs, the authors have been developing and evaluating a four element support program for interlock users in Alberta, Canada under a grant from the National Institute for Alcohol Abuse and Alcoholism (NIAAA, RO1-AA10320). This intervention is designed for application wherever interlock programs are employed. However, it is likely to be most effective in jurisdictions where judges require the interlock in lieu of more severe sanctions such as jail or house arrest so that most convicted DUIs will participate in the interlock program rather than suffer the unpleasant alternatives. This will draw into the interlock program more users who are less motivated to conform to the limitations of the interlock program and who therefore require more assistance to avoid interlock violations and to extend the safe behavior forced by the interlock into the period following its removal.

Intervention Overview. As part of the requirements for interlock use, offenders must visit the interlock service centers on a regular monthly or bimonthly basis in order to have their interlock equipment checked and recalibrated and to have their data recorder downloaded to disk, stored, and printed. This service visit provides the time and opportunity for an intervention that would otherwise not be fully used to best effect. Over the course of one year, there are seven to thirteen occasions when the offenders in Alberta must meet with the service providers.

During these visits, a four element program is currently being tested: (1) *educational support* to help offenders understand the operation and implications of driving with an interlock device in order to keep them in the interlock program; (2) *case management support* to assist the alcohol offenders to find (and use) community resources to facilitate their management of drinking or drinking-related health and social problems, at home or on the job; (3) *motivational enhancement therapy* to assist the heavy drinking offenders to acknowledge the need to evaluate their drinking and its consequences and to begin moving the offender along the readiness-to-change continuum; (4) *protective planning methods* to assist the offenders in developing plans that avoid the pitfalls of interlock use, such as becoming stranded because they are unable to start the engine after drinking.

The guiding model for the intervention is taken from Change Readiness Theory (Prochaska, DiClemente and Norcross, 1992). The behavior change that is being attempted is one that moves DUI offenders along a continuum of problem behavior recognition toward any one of several goals that are appropriate for different types of drinkers, ranging from abstinence-based treatment, to self-imposed moderation of drinking, to elimination of careless driving while drinking. In all cases, the objective (regardless of how achieved) is to reduce the public risk and personal harm associated with driving and alcohol use. The fifteen to twenty minutes available at the interlock service center is short but there is a body of literature to support the benefits of brief encounters.

(1) Educational Support Program. The Alberta experience has

shown educational support to actually be a desirable service to the offenders. Case managers play a significant role by demonstrating how to avoid penalties, explaining the link between the interlock centers and the driver control system (e.g., the Alberta Driver Control Board monitors compliance by reviewing findings of interlock violations), interpreting the printout from the interlock data recorder during each monthly visit to the interlock center, and by providing an emergency contact. During the visits, the case managers can determine whether the offender is having difficulty living within the program and can advise on methods for avoiding interlock "warns" and "fails" that can result in offenders being dropped from the program.

Most offenders recognize the self-interest in learning about how to avoid warns and fails because in addition to the punitive implications, their own inconvenience may be significant. For example, heavy drinkers may have a BAC > .04 in the morning after a drinking binge resulting in warns or fails when attempting to start the engine. The use of mouthwash and certain foods (if recently in the mouth) can also cause warns and fails. Very cold weather is often a problem for interlocks, and methods for pre-warming of the sampling head can be useful. These incidents are often useful discussion material for opening up a conversational relationship that can help move the offender along the change-readiness continuum toward lowering alcohol-related harm.

(2) Case Management Services. When the Alberta study began, an effort was made to use the occasion of regular service visits to refer clients to the available human service resources (Marques and Voas, 1995). This plan was based on the evidence that regular monitoring of DUI offenders has been shown to reduce recidivism (Reis, 1982; Voas and Tippetts, 1990). It was also based on the evidence that DUI offenders who are problem drinkers manifest a broad range of marital and job-related problems that might be reduced through human service agencies if the individual would accept referrals to such services. However, follow-through on referrals was often low as most offenders were found to be in very early alcohol problem recognition stages. It was found that for certain offenders, the case management referral functions were very useful when there was some willingness to acknowledge the existence of a

problem. In addition to the usual drug or alcohol treatment and family and vocational services, case managers also probe for the possibility of prior head injuries.

Research by Dennis Moore and his associates at Wright State has shown that among multiple DUI offenders, a high percentage (9.3%) have suffered traumatic brain injury at some point in the past that is exclusive of other learning disabilities and mental illness (Moore, Ford, & Li 1995). Moore's contention is that the evident failure to learn and adjust behavior after prior DUIs may be traceable to such chronic, often unrecognized, disability. Connecting such people to community resources for more in-depth evaluation may be helpful. In general, case management is most useful when a clear problem exists and the offender has some level of problem recognition–whether alcohol, family, or occupational–and will respond to the offer of assistance.

(3) Motivational Enhancement Therapy (MET). A number of alcohol treatment outcome studies have shown that length and intensity of treatment are not necessarily related to outcome (Annis, 1985; Miller & Hester, 1986). Under some circumstances, interventions as brief as one session compare favorably with traditional residential and outpatient treatment (Institute of Medicine, 1990; Oppenheimer, & Edwards, 1976). These favorable outcomes led to a number of studies of "brief interventions," and results have confirmed their effectiveness compared with no intervention controls and with more intense treatment programs (Babor, 1994; Bien, Miller, & Tonigan, 1993; Holder, Longabaugh, Miller, and Rubonis, 1991).

Motivational enhancement therapy (MET) was coined by Miller and Rollnick (1991) because one of the main ingredients of the brief intervention is "motivational." Six basic principles are believed to be critical: feedback about personal risk, clear advice to change, behavior change options, therapist empathy, an emphasis on the client's initiative for change, and a message of hope and self-efficacy (Miller & Sanchez, 1993). MET is a set of strategies to encourage people to seek treatment (Miller, 1996); it is a directive, client-centered approach for eliciting behavior change by helping clients explore and resolve ambivalence about change (Rollnick and Miller, 1995).

MET was adopted as an adjunctive to the case management approach used in Alberta because a high proportion of offenders were judged, in the parlance of the stage paradigm model of behavior change, to be in the "precontemplation" stage (Prochaska, DiClemente, and Norcross 1992; Prochaska, 1996). That stage is the tuned-out state of inattentiveness to a problem behavior, and the first of five behavior-change stages identified by the model: precontemplation, contemplation, preparation, action, and maintenance. Heather, Rollnick, Bell, and Richmond (1996) showed MET was more effective than skills approaches for those in the precontemplation and contemplation stages. The NIAAA Project MATCH (MATCH Research Group, 1997) study examined the effect of matching treatments to alcohol rehabilitation clients and found that more lengthy treatments offer little over MET, particularly in situations where clients are poorly motivated for change (such as those found in abundance among DUI offenders). The MATCH study also found MET to have more enduring effects over the longer term than the comparison cognitive behavioral treatment intervention (among clients lower on treatment-readiness criteria). It is the characteristic of change resistance that makes the alcohol offender difficult to reform. As a sample, the DUI offenders do not share many clinical characteristics with an alcohol treatment sample. For example, among the interlock DUI offenders in Alberta, only 4% of a sample of over 700 had Beck Depression Inventory scores above 16; by contrast approximately 25% of the MATCH study sample was over 16.

Several characteristics of MET make it appropriate to the interlock environment. First, the interviewers spend only a brief time (average 20 minutes) with the client at each monthly or bimonthly contact, so any intervention needs to be effective in a brief time. Second, the participants represent the full spectrum of drinking problems from newly abstinent to moderate, to highly dependent. The intervention has to be appropriate for diverse groups and be able to flexibly focus on whatever negotiable tactic will most reduce drinking and driving. Third, the case managers can encourage participants not only to reduce heavy drinking but also to make changes in other stressful and problematic life areas, assumed to have an indirect impact on drinking and driving decisions.

(4) Protective Planning Methods. McKnight et al. (1994) have demonstrated that a lack of planning in advance of attending drinking events is a major contributor to impaired driving. The goal behind providing support services in conjunction with an interlock program is to help offenders avoid DUI. The planning element is to convey advance thinking. Such planning may preclude becoming stranded without a ride (because BAC is too high to start car) or to avoid further costly DUI citations. Discussions with case managers include how to think about ride-share programs, (never assume there will be sober drivers at a drinking event willing to provide a ride home), anticipating high-risk situations (e.g., based on Marlatt's relapse prevention model), preplanning for a designated driver, and other ways to use planning to reduce exposure to high-risk situations. Cost calculations are done to assist the offender in appreciating the pragmatic implications of careless driving decisions.

CONCLUSION

The interlock technology is proving its value in reducing the risk that DUI offenders pose to the road-using public. It is a sanction that interferes as little as possible in the gainful employment of the offender and in the use of the vehicle by innocent family members. Finally, it has the potential advantage (unrealized to date) that by forcing "alcohol safe" driving behavior on the offender it may produce habits which will reduce harm after the interlock is removed. However, because most offenders will view the interlock as a burden and because participation involves some expense, courts will have to impose relatively severe alternative sentences to motivate most DUIs to install an interlock. The relatively lengthy period of interlock supervision (ranging from six months to several years) offers an unusual opportunity to intervene with individuals who have demonstrated a problem managing a balance between their drinking and driving. The alcohol intervention literature provides methods which are likely to be effective in assisting offenders to live within the limits imposed by interlock programs and assist them in gaining control over their drinking or drinking-driving. If

an interlock program accomplishes nothing more than keeping offenders from driving non-interlock vehicles for the period imposed
by the courts, the risk to the driving public will be substantially
reduced.

REFERENCES

Annis, H.M. (1985). Is inpatient rehabilitation of the alcoholic cost effective? Con
    position. *Advances in Alcohol and Substance Abuse, 5,* 175-190.
Babor, T.F. (1994). Avoiding the horrid and beastly sin of drunkenness: Does
    dissuasion make a difference? *Journal of Consulting and Clinical Psychology,
    62,* 1127-1140.
Beck, K.H., Rauch, W.J., & Baker, E.A. The Effects of Alcohol Ignition Interlock
    License Restrictions on Multiple Alcohol Offenders. A Randomized Trial in
    Maryland. Department of Psychology, University of Maryland, College Park,
    MD. In C. Mercier-Guyon (Ed.) *T'97 Alcohol, Drugs, and Traffic Safety. Vol. I,*
    177-183. Cermt, Annecy France.
Bien, T.H., Miller, W.R., & Tonigan, J.S. (1993). Brief interventions for alcohol
    problems. A review. *Addiction, 88,* 315-336.
Brewer, R.D., Morris, P.D., Cole, T.B., Watkins, S., Patetta, M.J., & Popkin, C.
    (1994). The risk of dying in alcohol-related automobile crashes among habitu-
    al drunk drivers. *New England Journal of Medicine, 331*(8).
Elliott, D.S., & Morse, B.J. (1993). *In-Vehicle BAC Test Devices as a Deterrent to
    DUI.* Final Report to the National Institute for Alcohol Abuse and Alcoholism.
Hagen, R.E. (1978). The efficacy of licensing controls as a countermeasure for
    multiple DUI offenders. *Journal of Safety Research* 10 (3): 115-122.
Heather, N., Rollnick, S., Bell, A., & Richmond, R. (1996). Effects of brief
    counseling among male heavy drinkers identified on general hospital wards.
    Drug & Alcohol Review, 15, 29-38.
Hedlund, J., and Fell, J. (1995) Persistent drinking drivers in the US. In *39th
    Annual proceedings of the AAAM*, pp. 1-12. Association for Automotive Medi-
    cine, Des Plaines, IL.
Holder, H., Longebaugh, R., Miller, W.R., & Rubonis, A.V. (1991). The cost-ef-
    fectiveness of treatment for alcoholism: A first approximation. *Journal of
    Studies on Alcohol, 52,* 517-540.
Institute of Medicine (1990). *Broadening the base of treatment for alcohol prob-
    lems.* Washington, D.C.: National Academy Press.
Jones, B. (1992). The effectiveness of Oregon's ignition interlock program. In:
    H.D. Utzelmann, G. Berghaus, and G. Kroj (eds.), *Alcohol, Drugs & Traffic
    Safety-T92*, Band 3: 1460-5. Cologne, Germany: Verleg TUV Rheinland.
Jones, R.K., Lacey, J.H., Berning, A., and Fell, J.C. (1996). Alternative sanctions
    for repeat DWI offenders. In: *40th Annual Proceedings of the Association for
    the Advancement of Automotive Medicine,* pp. 307-315. Des Plaines, IL:
    AAAM.

Marques, P.R., & Voas, R.B. (1995). Case-managed alcohol interlock programs: A bridge between the criminal and health systems. *Journal of Traffic Medicine, 23* (2).

Match Research Group. (1997). Matching Alcoholism Treatments to Client Heterogeneity: Project MATCH Post-Treatment Drinking Outcomes, *Journal of Studies on Alcohol,* Volume 58, Number 1, p. 7-29.

McKnight, A.J., Langston, E.A., McKnight, A.S., Resnick, J.A., & Lange, J.E. (1994). *Why people drink and drive: The basis of drinking-and-driving decisions.* (Contract No. DTNH22-91-C-07128). Washington, DC: National Highway Traffic Safety Administration.

McKnight, A.J., & Voas, R.B. (1991). The effect of license suspension upon DWI recidivism. *Alcohol, Drugs, & Driving, 7*(1).

Miller, W.R. (1996). Motivational interviewing: Research, practice and puzzles. *Addictive Behaviors, 21,* 835-842.

Miller, W.R., & Hester, R.K. (1986). The effectiveness of alcoholism treatment. In W.R. Miller & N. Heather (Eds.). *Treating Addictive Behaviors: Processes of Change.* New York: Plenum Press, pp 121-174.

Miller, W.R., & Rollnick, S. (1991). *Motivational interviewing. Preparing people to change addictive behavior.* New York: Guilford.

Miller, W.R., & Sanchez, V.C. (1993). Motivating young adults for treatment and lifestyle change. In Howard, G. (Ed.). *Issues in alcohol use and misuse by young adults.* Notre Dame, Indiana: University of Notre Dame Press.

Moore, D., Ford, J.A., & Li, L. (1995) The prevalence of disabilities among impaired drivers. In *Proceedings of 13th International Conference on Alcohol, Drugs and Traffic Safety,* Adelaide, Australia.

Nichols, J.L., & Ross, H.L. (1988). The effectiveness of legal sanctions in dealing with drinking drivers. In *The Surgeon Generals Workshop on Drunk Driving; Background Papers,* Washington, D.C.: Public Health Service, Office of the Surgeon General; 93-112.

Nichols, J.L., Weinstein, E., Ellingstad, V., & Struckman-Johnson, D. (1978). The specific deterrent effectiveness of ASAP education and rehabilitation programs. *Journal of Safety Research* 10 (4).

Peck, R.C., Sadler, D.D., & Perrine, M.W. (1985). The comparative effectiveness of alcohol rehabilitation and licensing control actions for drunk driving offenders: A review of the literature. *Alcohol, Drugs, and Driving; Abstracts and Reviews, 1* (4) ; 15-40.

Popkin, C.L., Stewart, J.R., Beckmeyer, J., and Martell, C. (1993). An evaluation of the effectiveness of interlock systems in preventing DWI recidivism among second-time DWI offenders. In: H.-D. Utzelmann, G. Berghaus, and G. Kroj (eds.), *Alcohol, Drugs & Traffic Safety-T92.* Cologne, Germany: Verlag TUV Rheinland, 3:1466-70.

Prochaska, J.O. (1996). A stage paradigm for integrating clinical and public health approaches to smoking cessation. *Addictive Behavior, 21,* 721-732.

Prochaska, J.O., DiClemente, C.C., & Norcross, J.C. (1992). In search of how people change: Applications to the addictive behaviors. *American Psychologist, 47,* 1102-1114.

Reis, R.E. (1982). *The Traffic Safety Effectiveness of Education Programs for Multiple Offense Drunk Drivers* (Contract No. HS-6-01414). Washington, DC: National Highway Traffic Safety Administration.

Rogers, A. (1994). Effect of Minnesota's license plate impoundment law on recidivism of multiple DWI violators. *Alcohol, Drugs & Driving,* Vol. 10, No. 2, 127-134.

Rollnick, S., & Miller, W.R. (1995). What is motivational interviewing? *Behavioral & Cognitive Psychotherapy, 23,* 325-334.

Sadler, D., & Perrine, M. (1984). *An Evaluation of the California Drunk Driving Countermeasure System: Volume 2, The Long-Term Traffic Safety Impact of a Pilot Alcoholic Abuse Treatment as an Alternative to License Suspensions.* Report No. 90. Sacramento, CA: Department of Motor Vehicles.

Simpson, H.M., Mayhew, D.R., Beirness, D.J. (1996). *Dealing with Hard Core Drinking Driver.* Traffic Injury Research Foundation. Ottawa, Canada. p 107.

Stewart, E.I., and Malfetti, J.L. (1970). *Rehabilitation of the Drunken Driver: A Corrective Course in Phoenix, Arizona, for Persons Convicted of Driving Under the Influence of Alcohol.* New York, NY.: Teachers College Press.

Tippetts, A.S., and Voas, R.B. (In Press). Impact of West Virginia Interlock Program on DUI recidivism. *Journal of Traffic Medicine.*

Voas, R.B.(1970). Cars That Drunks Can't Drive. Paper presented at the annual meeting of the Human Factors Society, San Francisco.

Voas, R.B., & Tippetts, A.S. (1990). Evaluation of treatment and monitoring programs for drunken drivers, *Journal of Traffic Medicine,* Volume 18, 15-26.

Voas, R.B., Tippetts, A.S., & Taylor E. (1997). Temporary Vehicle Immobilization: Evaluation of a Program in Ohio. *Accident Analysis and Prevention*, Vol. 29, No. 5, pp. 635-642.

Voas, R.B., Tippetts A.S., & Lange, J. (1997). Evaluation of a Method for Reducing Unlicensed Driving: The Washington and Oregon License Plate Sticker Laws. *Accident Analysis & Prevention,* Vol. 29, No. 5, pp. 627-634.

Voas, R.B., & Marques, P.R. (1992). *Alcohol Ignition Interlock Service Support.* (Contract No. DTNH22-89-C-07009). Washington DC: National Highway Safety Administration.

Voas, R.B., & McKnight, A.J. (1989). *An Evaluation of Hardship Licensing for DWIs.* (Contract No. DTNH22-34-C-07292). Washington, DC: National Highway Traffic Safety Administration.

Weinrath, M. (1997). The Ignition Interlock Program for Drunk Drivers: A Multivariate Test. *Crime and Delinquency,* Volume 43, No 1. January 97, 42-59.

Wells-Parker E. (1994). Mandated treatment: Lessons from research with drinking and driving offenders. *Alcohol Health & Research World, 18*(4), 302-306.

Wells-Parker, E., Bangert-Drowns, R., McMillen, D.L., & Williams, M. (1995). Final meta-analysis results of remedial interventions with drink/drive offenders. *Addiction.* 90; 907-926.

Wadda Ya Mean, I Can't Drive?:
Threat to Competence as a Factor in Drunk Driving Intervention

Elsie R. Shore
Kristi L. Compton
Wichita State University

SUMMARY. One method of preventing drunk driving is for people around the potential driver to intervene, but while research has provided information on prevalence, types, and effects of interventions, little attention has been given to theoretical constructs that might explain the behavior. The present study investigates the value of threat to competence as an explanatory concept. Five statements, determined to have different levels of threat to competence, were presented to college student volunteers (102 women, 99 men), who evaluated their potential effectiveness at stopping a friend from driving. As hypothesized, as level of threat increased, evaluations of effectiveness decreased. Implications for efforts to prevent drunk driving are discussed. *[Article copies available for a fee from The Haworth Document Delivery Service: 1-800-342-9678. E-mail address: getinfo@ haworth.com]*

INTRODUCTION

Driving while under the influence of alcohol (DUI) has been the focus of prevention activities for several decades. Formal deter-

---

The authors would like to thank Mary Wood for her assistance with this project, as well as her insightful comments.

[Haworth co-indexing entry note]: "*Wadda Ya Mean, I Can't Drive?*: Threat to Competence as a Factor in Drunk Driving Intervention." Shore, Elsie R., and Kristi L. Compton. Co-published simultaneously in *Journal of Prevention & Intervention in the Community* (The Haworth Press, Inc.) Vol. 17, No. 1, 1998, pp. 45-53; and: *Preventing Drunk Driving* (ed: Elsie R. Shore, and Joseph R. Ferrari) The Haworth Press, Inc., 1998, pp. 45-53. Single or multiple copies of this article are available for a fee from The Haworth Document Delivery Service [1-800-342-9678, 9:00 a.m. - 5:00 p.m. (EST). E-mail address: getinfo@haworth.com].

45

rence measures, such as changes in DUI laws, have had, at best, limited success (Hilton, 1984; Ross, 1984; Shore & Maguin, 1988). As a result, attention has turned to informal social control as a mechanism for reducing deaths and injuries, with the people around the impaired person increasingly being considered as possible intervenors in drunk driving situations.

Research on intervention to prevent an impaired person from driving has focused almost exclusively on the demographic characteristics of the individuals involved and on self-reported rates of intervention. Adebayo (1988) found that, among a random sample of adults in Edmonton, Canada, age was not a factor in the type of intervention the person reportedly would choose. Similarly, in a sample of college students, Monto, Newcomb, Rabow, and Hernandez (1992) found that the age of the intervenor in relation to that of the target person did not affect likelihood of intervention. Race, gender, and marital status have not been found to influence intervention likelihood or technique, although intervenors and target persons were more likely to be of the same gender and race (Adebayo, 1988; Monto et al., 1992). Hernandez, Newcomb, and Rabow (1995) also found few gender differences in types and frequency of intervention, in a college sample. In a study of DUI offenders, however, Pandiani and McGrath (1986) found that women, those with higher BACs, and those exhibiting fearful or anxious behaviors were more likely to be targets of intervention attempts. They found that older people also were more likely to be targets of intervention.

These and other studies of informal drunk driving prevention activities and intervenors have provided much worthwhile information. What is largely missing, however, is the development of theories that might provide a context in which intervention behavior and outcomes can be better understood. Considering intervention as a helping behavior seems intuitively correct, but the act of intervening in a drunk driving situation does not easily fit traditional helping paradigms (Newcomb, Rabow, Monto, & Hernandez, 1991; Rabow, Newcomb, Monto, & Hernandez, 1990; Hernández et al., 1995). Monto et al. (1992) found evidence to support both social status and intervenor-target similarity as affecting intervention. Pandiani and McGrath (1986) considered two ways of interpreting their findings with regard to more likely target persons for prevention attempts. They suggested that women, older people, and those with higher BACs might be more likely targets because they are perceived to be less self-sufficient, or because it is less socially costly to intervene with them. The social cost of intervention is the possibility of rejection of the offer, resulting from a perceived "challenge to the potential driver's manhood, adulthood, or overall social competence" (p. 347).

The work of Gusfield and colleagues might provide a useful basis for theory development. These researchers focused on competence as an important aspect of the drinking-driving issue (Gusfield, 1979; Gusfield, 1985; Gusfield, Kotarba, & Rasmussen, 1981). In an ethnographic study of bars, they found that the competent man was one who is able to drink with his group *and* able to drive afterward. Women, the young, and the old were seen as exempt from this expectation; they could relinquish or be relieved of driving responsibilities without feeling the loss of face an adult man would experience.

Intimates such as friends and spouses are expected to help the male drinker maintain a competent "front" before others in the bar. Their close relationship to the drinker also, however, requires them to keep him safe, which may involve preventing him from driving. One way that intimates, especially spouses, balanced these two roles was to act, in the bar, as if the impaired person would be driving, but, when out of sight, to take over (Gusfield, 1979; Gusfield et al., 1981).

The concept of threat to competence as related to the prevention of drunk driving has occasionally been discussed, but it has not been systematically investigated. The purpose of the present project was to assess the applicability of Gusfield and colleagues' observations to theory development and understanding of the drunk driving intervention situation. It was hypothesized that the threat level of statements made to persuade a person to refrain from driving would correlate with perceptions of the effectiveness of the statements such that as threat increased, perceived effectiveness would decrease.

METHOD

Participants

Two hundred and one student volunteers (102 females, 99 males) enrolled in introduction psychology classes at a public, Midwestern university received research credit for their participation in this study. The mean age was 22.2 years; the age range (16 to 50 years) reflects the nontraditional nature of the university's student population. The majority of the participants spoke English as their native language (86.1%), drank more than one alcoholic drink per year (78.1%), and had never been charged with driving while intoxicated (96.5%). Most had at some time tried to stop a friend from driving after drinking (70.6%); fewer (38.0%) reported ever having had anyone try to stop them.

Instruments

Participants were asked to judge five statements, each presenting a sentence that could be used to stop someone who had been drinking from driving. The statements were chosen from an earlier study, in which students were asked to assess sixteen sentences for their threat to competence, defined as an action or statement that calls into question the ability of a person to perform adequately or to perform up to expectations. A four point scale, from not threatening to very threatening, was used. Each statement began with the same phrase, "How about if I drive," followed by a different ending. The endings, chosen to reflect a range of threat levels (Table 1), were: " . . . I've heard that the police are really looking for DUIs," " . . . you've had too much," " . . . you're really drunk," " . . . you're smashed," and " . . . you're going to get us both killed."

Procedure

Participants were asked to imagine the following situation, in which the potential driver probably should not drive:

> You and a friend are at a party. Your friend drove the two of you there. While you have had very little to drink, your friend

has had enough so that he or she is probably over the legal limit for DUI. As the two of you get ready to leave the party, you turn to your friend and say something.

They then were asked to read the five statements and choose the one they thought would be most likely to persuade their friend to turn over the keys. In order to avoid a mechanical approach to the task, the students were next asked to choose the statement they felt would be *least* likely to persuade their friend; the remaining three statements were chosen in order of decreasing perceived effectiveness. A questionnaire asking for demographic and other information was completed and the respondents were debriefed concerning the purposes of the study.

The above procedure was chosen in order to decrease potential social desirability effects. At the present time, stopping someone from driving is seen by many as reflecting positively on the intervenor ("Friends don't let friends drive drunk"). By asking respondents to rank rather than to rate or choose statements, we hoped to avoid evoking respondents' desire to display their social consciousness, thus keeping them focused on the statements themselves.

TABLE 1. Perceived Effectiveness of Stimulus Sentences

Stimulus Sentence	Threat Level	Rating		Rating – Females		Rating – Males	
		N = 201		N = 101		N = 99	
	$\bar{x}$	$\bar{x}$	(s.d.)	$\bar{x}$	(s.d.)	$\bar{x}$	(s.d.)
. . . Police	2.18	3.76	(1.46)	4.05	(1.20)	3.45	(1.64)
. . . Too much	2.39	3.28	(1.33)	3.34	(1.39)	3.21	(1.27)
. . . Really Drunk	3.36	2.75	(1.10)	2.59	(1.07)	2.91	(1.12)
. . . Smashed	3.45	2.40	(1.20)	2.11	(1.09)	2.71	(1.24)
. . . Killed	3.79	2.80	(1.54)	2.91	(1.48)	2.68	(1.59)

RESULTS

The average effectiveness rating (i.e., rating of likelihood that the statement would prevent the person from driving) of each sentence is presented in Table 1, along with each *a priori* determined threat rating. A two-way analysis of variance (gender × statement) yielded a significant main effect for statement ($F(4, 1.90) = 7.41, p < .01$). The gender and interaction effects were not statistically significant. With the exception of the "You're really drunk" vs. "You're going to get us both killed" comparison, the means of all the other pairs of effectiveness ratings reached statistically significant levels.

Among the men the correlation between threat and effectiveness ratings was statistically significant and inverse ($r_s = -1.00$, p < .01), such that as threat level increased, perceived effectiveness decreased. Among the women, and for both genders combined, the correlations also were inverse and approached a statistically significant level ($r_s = -.70$, p = .09). Participants were grouped by drinking status (drinkers, abstainers), whether they ever had tried to intervene with a friend, whether someone had ever tried to stop them from driving after drinking, and by native language (English, non-English). Statistically significant correlations between effectiveness ratings and threat were found for drinkers ($r_s = -.90$, p = .02), for those who reported that someone had tried to stop them ($r_s = -.90$, p = .02), and for those whose native language was not English ($r_s = -.80$, p = .05). All the other correlations were inverse as well, and all approached but did not attain statistically significant levels (all $r_s = -.70$, p = .09).

The sentence stating that the potential driver will "get us both killed" was the only one that changed position when different groupings were considered. Among men, that statement was rated fifth; women rated it third. In all other subgroups the mean ratings placed the statement third or fourth. Removing that statement resulted in perfect inverse correlations between threat and effectiveness ratings for all subgroups, with the invariant order being "Police," "Had too much," "Really drunk," and "Smashed."

DISCUSSION

The hypothesis that threat to competence is related to partici-pants' choices of intervention statements was supported by the data. As level of threat increased, sentences were rated as less likely to be effective in stopping a friend from driving after drinking. The sen-tence chosen as most effective made no direct reference to the person targeted for intervention, while the effectiveness ratings of three others decreased as the statement about the person became more severe and direct.

The interpretation offered here, in agreement with Gusfield et al. (1986), is that statements attacking the person's sense of compe-tence are perceived to violate the requirement that a friend preserve his/her friend's "face," even while trying to protect that friend from harm. Perhaps, in addition, personally threatening statements are perceived as likely to produce arguments and other forms of resis-tance. Thus, by shifting the focus away from the impaired person, the intervenor maintains the social contract between friends and expedites the process of preventing the person from driving. The impaired person, in turn, can ignore the relatively obvious, *but unstated,* judgment of incompetence and turn over the keys without feeling the need to stage a protest.

The exception to the exact inverse correlation between threat and effectiveness was the "you're going to get us both killed" sentence. The average for male respondents placed the statement at the bot-tom of the effectiveness ratings, while the female average placed it in the middle. Other subgroup differences (i.e., drinking status, experience with drunk driving situations) may be a function of the men's and women's different perceptions of this statement.

It is important to reiterate, however, that the relative rankings of the four other statements were the same for male and female re-spondents. This suggests that men and women are more alike than different in their response to the threat level of intervention state-ments. This gender similarity is supported by research showing that men and women respond similarly to other aspects of drunk driving intervention situations (Adebayo, 1988; Monto et al., 1992).

The results of this study suggest that threat to competence may be an important factor to consider when planning programs to increase informal efforts to stop drunk drivers. Interventions that attribute the need to refrain from driving to external sources (e.g., police, possibility of DUI) are less confrontive than those that emphasize the impaired state of the potential driver. These and other less confrontive approaches might be more acceptable to the potential intervenor and to the target person, thus making them more likely to be used and more likely to be effective. Prevention strategies might include training both private citizens and restaurant and bar personnel to intervene without threatening the target person's "face," and using media campaigns to provide models of nonthreatening interactions, communication techniques suggested earlier by Pandiani and McGrath (1986).

This study represents the first attempt to test the concept of threat to competence as a factor in informal intervention to prevent drunk driving. More research is needed, to replicate and to extend these findings. Participants in this study appear to believe that some statements (e.g., those with lower threat levels) are more effective; a next step would be to investigate whether less threatening statements are, in fact, more effective in preventing drunk driving. Other research may further clarify the role threat to competence plays, and offer additional suggestions for the improvement of drunk driving prevention activities.

REFERENCES

Adebayo, A. (1988). Drunk-driving intervention in an urban community: An exploratory analysis. *British Journal of Addiction, 83,* 423-429.

Collins, M. D., & Frey, J. H. (1992). Drunken driving and informal social control: The case of peer intervention. *Deviant Behavior: An Interdisciplinary Journal, 13,* 73-87.

Gusfield, J. R. (1979). Managing competence: An ethnographic study of drinking-driving and the context of bars. In Harford, T. C. & Gaines, L. S. (Eds.) *Social drinking contexts.* Research Monograph #7, USDHHS, NIAAA, Rockville, MD.

Gusfield, J. R. (1985) Social and cultural contexts of the drinking-driving event. *Journal of Studies on Alcohol,* Supplement #10, 70-77.

Gusfield, J. R., Kotarba, J., & Rasmussen, P. (1981). The public society of intimates: Friends, wives, lovers and others in the drinking-driving drama. *Research in the interweave of social roles: Friendship, 2,* 237-257.

Hernández, A. C. R., Newcomb, M. D., & Rabow, J. (1995). Types of drunk-driving intervention: Prevalence, success and gender. *Journal of Studies on Alcohol, 56*(4), 408-413.

Hilton, M. (1984). The impact of recent changes in California drinking-driving law on fatal accident levels during the first post-intervention year. *Law and Society Review, 18,* 605-628.

Monto, M. A., Newcomb, M. D., Rabow, J., & Hernandez, A. C. R. (1992). Social status and drunk-driving intervention. *Journal of Studies on Alcohol, 53*(1), 63-68.

Newcomb, M. D., Rabow, J., Monto, M. A., & Hernandez, A. C. R. (1991). Informal drunk driving intervention: Psychosocial correlates among young adult women and men. *Journal of Applied Social Psychology, 21,* 1988-2006.

Pandiani, J., & McGrath, R. J. (1986). Attempts to dissuade drinkers from driving: The effect of driver characteristics. *Journal of Drug Education, 16*(4), 341-348.

Rabow, J., Hernandez, A. C. R., & Watts, R. K. (1986). College students do intervene in drunk driving situations. *Sociology and Social Research, 70*(3), 224-225.

Rabow, J., Newcomb, M. D., Monto, M. A., & Hernandez, A. C. R. (1990). Altruism in drunk driving situations: Personal and situational factors in intervention. *Social Psychology Quarterly, 53*(3), 199-213.

Ross, H. L. (1984). *Deterring the drinking driver: Legal policy and social control* Lexington, MA: D.C. Heath & Co.

Shore, E.R., & Maguin, E. (1988). Deterrence of drinking driving: The effects of changes in the Kansas Driving Under the Influence Law. *Evaluation Research and Planning, 11,* 245-254.

A Community-Based Feedback Process for Disseminating Pedestrian BAC Levels

Kent E. Glindemann
E. Scott Geller
Steven W. Clarke
Candice R. Chevaillier
Charles B. Pettinger, Jr.

Center for Applied Behavior Systems

SUMMARY. During National Collegiate Alcohol Awareness Weeks of 1992, 1994, and 1995, blood alcohol concentration (BAC) feedback was offered to pedestrians. Two BAC feedback stations were set up near bars frequented by many university students, and were staffed for either two or three consecutive nights. These stations provided passers-by with their BAC, as determined by portable breathalyzers. Across the three years of the study, a total of 1,590 individuals (1,192 men, 398 women) participated. The mean BAC for all participants was 0.063 (S.D. = 0.039), ranging from 0.0 to 0.310. Data analysis revealed a main effect for BAC across days, with average BAC being significantly greater on Thursdays than Fridays. A main effect was also found for time, with BACs becoming higher as the night progressed. No main effect for gender was found. However, a significant gender by day of the week interaction resulted from female BAC levels being higher than those of males on Thursdays

This research was partially supported by research grants to E. Scott Geller (principal investigator) from the National Institute on Alcohol Abuse and Alcoholism (5 R01 AA09604-02) and the Alcoholic Beverage Medical Research Foundation.

[Haworth co-indexing entry note]: "A Community-Based Feedback Process for Disseminating Pedestrian BAC Levels." Glindemann, Kent E. et al. Co-published simultaneously in *Journal of Prevention & Intervention in the Community* (The Haworth Press, Inc.) Vol. 17, No. 1, 1998, pp. 55-68; and: *Preventing Drunk Driving* (ed: Elsie R. Shore, and Joseph R. Ferrari) The Haworth Press, Inc., 1998, pp. 55-68. Single or multiple copies of this article are available for a fee from The Haworth Document Delivery Service [1-800-342-9678, 9:00 a.m. - 5:00 p.m. (EST). E-mail address: getinfo@haworth.com].

but male BAC levels being higher than those of females on Fridays. Implications of findings for intervention efforts aimed at curtailing DUI and other alcohol-related problems are discussed. *[Article copies available for a fee from The Haworth Document Delivery Service: 1-800-342-9678. E-mail address: getinfo@haworth.com]*

Alcohol abuse among young adults and accompanying undesirable behaviors (e.g., physical aggressiveness, vandalism, date rape, driving under the influence of alcohol) represent a significant public health problem (Laurence, Snortum, & Zimring, 1988). Although the use of alcohol is illegal for anyone under the age of 21, it remains more widespread among youth than the use of tobacco or any illicit drug. Among college students alcohol is more than twice as popular as both tobacco and marijuana, and almost nine times more popular than cocaine. Further, between 80-90% of college students report having used alcohol while in college (Johnston, 1990). Wechsler and colleagues found that approximately 84% of college students reported consuming alcohol within the last year (Wechsler, Davenport, Dowdall, Moeykens, & Castillo, 1994). Of those students, 44% were considered binge drinkers (defined as consuming five or more drinks per bout for men, and four or more drinks for women, once a week or more), and 19% overall were considered frequent binge drinkers.

Despite the finding that DUI has gradually decreased among college students (Engs & Hanson, 1988), it remains a dangerous problem on today's highways. A driver with a blood alcohol concentration (BAC) of 0.05 is about twice as likely to be involved in a fatal traffic crash as a driver who has not consumed any alcoholic beverage (Sleet, Wagenaar, & Waller, 1989). It is possible a considerable percentage of these road crashes could be avoided by providing people the opportunity to receive BAC feedback before they get behind the wheel of an automobile. Unfortunately, traditional approaches to addressing DUI have focused on either apprehending drunks while behind the wheel or obtaining legal convictions after an alcohol-related crash (Geller, Kalsher, & Clarke, 1991). A proactive approach should focus on curtailing DUI *before* potential drivers get behind the wheel of a car.

The purpose of this research was twofold: to increase community awareness of impairment from alcohol consumption, and to collect epidemiological data on students' alcohol consumption and impairment in a naturalistic setting.

NATIONAL COLLEGIATE ALCOHOL AWARENESS WEEK

More than 3,000 universities in the United States, Canada, and Mexico participate in National Collegiate Alcohol Awareness Week (NCAAW) during the third week of October. The purpose of NCAAW is to: (a) educate students about the potential dangers of alcohol use and abuse, (b) inform students of various alternative activities to drinking, and (c) increase students' awareness of responsible choices regarding the consumption of alcohol (BAC-CHUS, 1996).

Combining the provision of community service with the opportunity to collect useful epidemiological data, we offered BAC feedback to pedestrians during NCAAW. We staffed two BAC feedback stations for consecutive nights during three university-supported NCAAWs occurring in the Fall of 1992, 1994, and 1995. The stations were located in the vicinity of bars frequented by many university students. The BAC feedback stations used portable breathalyzers to provide passers-by with their level of intoxication. The stations also provided information on alcohol use and abuse, as well as schedules for the local public transportation system. The data collected during this community service activity included the BAC and gender of the participant, and the day, time, and year of each BAC assessment.

METHOD

Participants and Setting

The Town of Blacksburg, a community of about 35,000 people, is located in the mountains of southwestern Virginia. Virginia Tech, a land-grant university located in Blacksburg, is composed of approximately 19,000 undergraduate students, 4,800 graduate students, and 5,500 faculty and staff members.

A total of 1,590 individuals (1,192 men, 398 women) participated across the three years of this project. The participants totaled 421 in 1992 (361 men, 60 women), 369 in 1994 (277 men, 92 women), and 800 in 1995 (554 men, 246 women). Most participants were Virginia Tech students (83%), although any willing pedestrian was included in the sample.

For all three years, the two BAC feedback stations were set up on Thursday and Friday nights from 4:00 pm to 3:00 am. In 1995, the stations were also in place on Wednesday night. The two stations were located on the sidewalks of separate downtown streets in the vicinity of popular bars (n = 14).

Materials

Each station included an $8' \times 3'$ table and four chairs. Posters announcing the availability of BAC feedback were displayed to attract attention. Various pamphlets were available, containing information about alcohol and the consequences of alcohol abuse, as well as bumper stickers with anti-DUI slogans (donated from the University Student Health Services). In addition, bus schedules and taxi cards were displayed to assist drinkers in finding safe transportation home. Two to four student research assistants were present at each station to administer the BAC tests.

BAC Measurement. Participant BAC levels were assessed using hand-held Alco-Sensor III breathalyzers (Intoximeters Inc., St. Louis, MO). Four breathalyzer units (accuracy $= +/- .005$ BAC) were available at each station. Before submitting a breath sample, participants were asked to swish about 2 oz of water in their mouth to remove any residual alcohol. A standardized sampling procedure was used to ensure alveolar (i.e., deep lung) air was collected. All instruments were calibrated annually by the Blacksburg Police Department.

Community Resources. Each year, outside support was sought from various organizations in the community. Permission to set up and operate the stations was granted by both the town manager and the local Chief of Police. Also, the Chief of Police was asked to inform his patrol officers of the project so they would not unduly interfere with the BAC feedback process and "scare away" potential participants. Next, support was sought from the University Student Health Services (USHS). This organization was brought aboard as a co-sponsor of the project, and each year they were able to supply pamphlets, brochures, and other materials for distribution to participants. In addition, the USHS integrated this project with other activities sponsored by the university during NCAAW, and provided publicity to university students regarding the availability of the BAC feedback.

Procedure

When potential participants approached one of the BAC feedback stations, they were asked if they would like to have their intoxication measured. If they agreed, the purpose of the study was briefly explained. They were then asked to read and sign an informed consent form which outlined the study, emphasized the confidentiality of the data, and indicated the study had been approved by the Human Subjects Committee and Institutional Review Board of the University, as well as the Blacksburg Police Department. After signing the consent form, participants were asked questions assessing their age, gender, and the specific quantity of alcohol consumed so far that night.

After the brief interview, participants were asked if they had consumed an alcoholic beverage within the last 15 minutes. If they had, water was provided to rinse any residual alcohol from their mouth. Then they were instructed to "take a deep breath and blow as long and hard as you can through the tube," and administered a BAC test with a breathalyzer. The reading was recorded on a data sheet (along with the date and time of the test) and confidentially given to the participant. The participant's hand was then marked with an indelible marker, enabling researchers to keep track of those who had their BAC assessed. This was performed to prevent participants from receiving BAC feedback more than once. Finally, each participant was thanked for participating and verbally discouraged from driving if they had consumed any alcohol.

RESULTS

The BACs were examined by levels of year, day, time, and gender. Time was divided into three mutually exclusive intervals: 4:00 pm to 7:59 pm (representing "happy hour" drinking), 8:00 pm to

11:59 pm (nighttime drinking), and 12:00 am to 3:00 am (late night drinking). Mean BACs and sample sizes are presented in Table 1 by levels of year, day, time interval, and gender.

A 3 Year (1992, 1994, 1995) × 3 Day (Wednesday, Thursday, Friday) × 3 Time Interval (Happy Hour, Night, Late Night) × 2 Gender (Men, Women) Analysis of Variance (ANOVA) was performed on the dependent variable (BAC). Main effects were obtained for Day, $F (2, 1550) = 4.0$ ($p < .05$), and Time Interval, $F (2, 1550) = 5.68$ ($p < .01$).

The Day × Time Interval interaction reached significance, $F (4, 1550) = 2.72$ ($p < .05$). As depicted in Figure 1, BACs started relatively low but rose progressively throughout the night on Wednesdays and Thursdays; but on Fridays, mean BAC started at a moderate level and remained relatively stable.

The Year × Time Interval interaction also reached significance, $F (4, 1550) = 2.91$ ($p < .05$). In 1992, BACs were lowest during the Night and Late Night periods. In 1994, BACs were highest for all Time Intervals, while in 1995 BACs were lowest during Happy Hour.

The Day × Gender interaction approached significance, $F (2, 1550) = 2.41$ ($p = .09$), and is illustrated in Figure 2. The data for Wednesday, however, were obtained only in 1995. The 2 Day (Thursday, Friday) × 2 Gender (Men, Women) ANOVA revealed a significant Day × Gender interaction, $F (1, 1480) = 9.35$ ($p < .01$). This interaction resulted from female BAC levels being higher than those of males on Thursdays but male BAC levels being higher than those of females on Fridays.

No other main effects nor interactions approached significance (all $ps > .10$).

DISCUSSION

The current study provided BAC feedback to pedestrians in a university community during NCAAW, and at the same time collected substantial epidemiological data on student alcohol consumption and intoxication. The community service aspect of this project was well received, and is feasible for numerous communi-

TABLE 1. Mean: BAC and Sample Size by Year, Day, Gender, and Time.

Year	Day	Happy Hour Men	Happy Hour Women	Night Men	Night Women	Late Night Men	Late Night Women	Total Men	Total Women	Total Total
1992	Thursday	.059 (8)	.071 (1)	.065 (108)	.079 (18)	.076 (50)	.065 (8)	.067 (161)	.072 (27)	.069 (193)
	Friday	.062 (78)	.051 (15)	.054 (82)	.057 (13)	.063 (35)	.093 (5)	.060 (195)	.067 (33)	.063 (228)
	Total	.061 (86)	.061 (16)	.060 (190)	.068 (31)	.070 (85)	.079 (13)	.063 (361)	.069 (60)	.066 (421)
1994	Thursday	.011 (2)	–	.072 (66)	.104 (18)	.087 (49)	.105 (27)	.056 (117)	.105 (45)	.076 (162)
	Friday	.066 (63)	.048 (7)	.063 (81)	.055 (31)	.073 (16)	.053 (9)	.067 (160)	.052 (47)	.060 (207)
	Total	.083 (65)	.048 (7)	.068 (147)	.080 (49)	.080 (65)	.079 (36)	.062 (277)	.079 (92)	.067 (369)
1995	Wednesday	.024 (11)	–	.080 (39)	.052 (24)	.080 (91)	.088 (41)	.061 (141)	.070 (65)	.065 (206)
	Thursday	.051 (15)	.021 (9)	.067 (82)	.061 (42)	.085 (150)	.083 (70)	.068 (247)	.055 (121)	.061 (368)
	Friday	.057 (43)	.042 (16)	.063 (72)	.040 (28)	.066 (51)	.063 (16)	.062 (166)	.048 (60)	.055 (226)
	Total	.044 (69)	.032 (25)	.070 (193)	.051 (94)	.077 (292)	.078 (127)	.064 (554)	.056 (246)	.060 (800)
Total	Wednesday	.024 (11)	–	.080 (39)	.052 (24)	.080 (91)	.088 (41)	.061 (141)	.070 (65)	.065 (206)
	Thursday	.040 (25)	.046 (10)	.068 (256)	.081 (78)	.083 (249)	.084 (105)	.064 (530)	.070 (193)	.067 (723)
	Friday	.062 (184)	.047 (38)	.060 (235)	.051 (72)	.067 (102)	.070 (30)	.063 (521)	.056 (140)	.061 (661)
	Total	.047 (220)	.047 (48)	.066 (530)	.064 (174)	.076 (442)	.079 (176)	.063 (1192)	.065 (398)	.063 (1590)

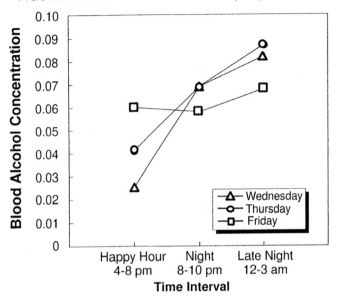

FIGURE 1. Mean BAC of Pedestrians by Day and Time Interval

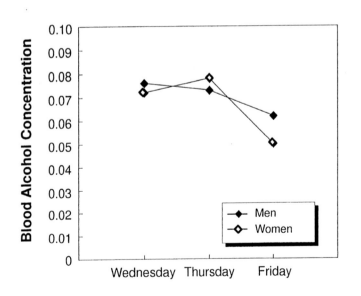

FIGURE 2. Mean BAC of Pedestrians by Day and Gender

ties as a way to increase community awareness of the dangers of alcohol abuse. Over the course of three years, BAC feedback was provided to over 1,500 pedestrians. And the pedestrians' reactions to this service were overwhelmingly positive. Many participants commented on how they had always wanted to have their BAC assessed so they could match a quantitative or "legal" number to their internal feelings of impairment. Others indicated it was "cool" and "fun." Also, the BAC feedback stations fit in well with the educational activities already planned by the USHS for NCAAW, and added a research component to those efforts. As a result, we collected a wealth of data while performing this community service.

Gender Differences

The failure to find a main effect for differences in intoxication levels between men and women was surprising, given the documentation of gender differences in collegiate alcohol use (Berkowitz & Perkins, 1986; Engs & Hanson, 1985, 1989). In college populations, men have been consistently found to drink more frequently and in greater quantities than women, and to experience more alcohol-related problems (Perkins, 1992). However, these studies have all relied on self-reported accounts of alcohol use rather than actual BAC levels, and this may account for the discrepancy between these previous findings and our own. It could be that men are more willing to admit alcohol abuse than women, thus accounting for gender differences in verbal report data.

In support of our findings, other assessments of actual BAC among college students have also failed to find a main effect of gender. Specifically, research we conducted in fraternity party settings in 1995 failed to show BAC differences between men and women when they left the parties (Geller & Glindemann, 1996; Glindemann, Geller, & Fortney, 1997). Overall, the mean exit BAC for men was .098 (SD = .06), ranging from .00 to .226, and the mean exit BAC for women was .089 (SD = .07), ranging from .00 to .194. Additional research is needed to determine whether our findings are indicative of a disappearing gender effect regarding drinking patterns, which is not readily detected with self-report data.

Day of Week

For each year, average BAC was significantly greater on Thursday than Friday. At many colleges and universities, Thursday night has become a major social night for students, and our findings indicate alarmingly high intoxication levels on this night. Given that many students have classes on Fridays, this trend is cause for concern. It could result in decreased class attendance or academic performance on Fridays by those students consuming alcohol on Thursday nights.

Our results, however, are contrary to those of previous research. Arfken (1988), using a national sample from the general U.S. population, found *self-reported* drinking rates to be highest on Friday and Saturday night. Further, their results showed Thursday night drinking patterns to be no different than other weekday nights. Differences between Arfken's findings and those reported here may be due to characteristics of the sample populations measured. It is probable that student drinking patterns differ from those of the general population in significant ways, and our findings reflect these differences. Also, the earlier research relied on self-reported measures of drinking rates rather than actual intoxication levels, and this could account for some discrepancies.

Time of Day

As expected, mean BAC rose progressively throughout the night, with mean BAC being lowest during the happy hour interval and highest during the late night interval. These results are in line with the self-report data of Orcutt (1993) and Orcutt and Harvey (1991), who found drinking among college students to be greater during an 8 pm - midnight time block than a 4 pm to 8 pm time block. It should be pointed out that our time intervals were not necessarily mutually exclusive for participants. Drinkers in the late night condition may well have been consuming alcohol since the beginning of happy hour, and as such, their greater level of intoxication may merely be due to the fact they had consumed a greater number of drinks over a greater time span. Nevertheless, our results reflect intoxication levels of pedestrians at the time they were sampled, and, overall, these intoxication levels were highest during the late night time interval. This indicates that interventions to prevent DUI are most needed during the late night period.

Day by Time Interval

During happy hour, BAC levels were significantly higher on Fridays than on Wednesdays or Thursdays. On Wednesdays and Thursdays however, BAC levels rose progressively through the night, while remaining virtually stable throughout the night on Fridays (see Figure 1). This finding of increased BAC levels during happy hour on Fridays may reflect differences in reasons for alcohol consumption. Friday afternoons typically signify the end of the work week or school week, and research has indicated that many individuals drinking during this time frame consume alcohol to relieve the stress and tension of the week, rather than for more social reasons (Orcutt, 1993; Orcutt & Harvey, 1991). Again, however, it should be pointed out that these results do not take into consideration how long a participant had been drinking. It is possible some participants were consuming alcohol through all three time intervals on Wednesday and Thursday nights, thus precipitating higher late night BACs. Conversely, the data across the three time intervals on Friday nights could reflect the BAC levels of different groups of drinkers out for shorter periods of time. Additional research is needed to resolve this potential confound.

Day by Gender

On Thursdays, female BAC levels were higher than those of males. On Fridays, however, male BAC levels were higher than those of females (see Figure 2). Additionally, BAC levels for women were highest on Thursdays. These differences in the drinking patterns of men and women could have implications for the best days of the week to plan interventions aimed at preventing DUI and other alcohol-related problems. These data, for example, indicate that women are more at-risk for alcohol-related problems on Thursdays than Fridays. As such, interventions aimed specifically at women may do better to concentrate prevention efforts on this day of the week.

Limitations of the Research and Implications for Future Studies

There are several limitations to this research. It is important to consider that our sample was self-selected and not random. Only those who approached one of the BAC feedback stations to have their BAC assessed participated in this project. It may be that these people possess qualities which make them non-representative of all college students or the general population. Future research should include a test of this BAC dissemination procedure using a random sample.

Another limitation is that data were only collected during NCAAW. It may be that drinking rates among college students are significantly different during NCAAW than at other times of the year. In fact, it is hoped that BACCHUS, GAMMA, and many student health organizations reach students with their message during this week, and that drinking rates are lower during NCAAW than at other times of the year. This is a frightening consideration, however, given the relatively high BACs observed. Future research should obtain BACs at times other than during NCAAW. This would accomplish two purposes. First, it would verify the veracity of the results reported here. Second, and more importantly, it would provide a direct test of the impact of NCAAW activities on student drinking rates, and perhaps suggest directions for future prevention activities.

An additional limitation of this research is that it included no test of intervention effectiveness. It is unknown whether this BAC feedback procedure had any effect on participants' subsequent alcohol consumption or alcohol-impaired driving. Nevertheless, it is possible the data could be useful when developing future interventions for curtailing DUI. Arfken (1988) posited that an assessment of injuries caused by alcohol must take into account when people are drinking. An identification of the days and times during which students are most likely to be impaired or intoxicated could have practical benefits for the implementation of prevention interventions. This strategy is termed "market segmentation" in the realm of social marketing, and is often the first step in a large-scale campaign to change behaviors or attitudes (Geller, 1989; Glindemann, Geller, & Ludwig, 1996). The data reported here, for example, indicate that an ideal time to intervene on college students (especially co-eds) consuming alcohol would be late Thursday nights.

For maximum impact, DUI-prevention interventions should be enacted at the time and place where DUI is most likely to occur (Geller, Winett, & Everett, 1982). The field data of the present study is instructional regarding the days and times interventions aimed at curtailing DUI among college and university students should be implemented. The research also sets precedent for supplementing verbal report surveys with actual field observations of drinking behaviors and intoxication levels. Indeed, our observations indicate an alarming number of both male and female university students are intoxicated on these weeknights and at risk for DUI. What was previously learned from verbal report data was verified by direct field observation, except the presumption that the problem is greater for male than female students was disconfirmed.

AUTHOR NOTE

Data collection was assisted by Jason N. Fortney, Amy B. Gershenoff, Paul G. Michael, Mary L. Spiller, Jamie M. Spisak, Kristy L. Maddox, and Jason P. DePasquale, among others. Special thanks are extended to Carolyn T. Penn of Virginia Tech's Student Health Services, and to the Blacksburg Police Department. Address correspondence to Kent E. Glindemann or E. Scott Geller, Center for Applied Behavior Systems, Department of Psychology, Virginia Tech, Blacksburg, Virginia 24061-0436.

REFERENCES

Arfken, C.L. (1988). Temporal pattern of alcohol consumption in the United States. *Alcoholism Clinical Experiments and Research, 12,* 137-142.

BACCHUS (1996). *National Collegiate Alcohol Awareness Week Programming Manual.* Denver, CO: The BACCHUS & GAMMA Peer Education Network.

Berkowitz, A.D., & Perkins, H.W. (1986). Problem drinking among college students: A review of recent research. *Journal of American College Health, 35,* 21-28.

Engs, R.C., & Hanson, D.J. (1985). The drinking patterns and problems of college students: 1983. *Journal of Alcohol and Drug Education, 31,* 65-85.

Engs, R.C., & Hanson, D.J. (1988). University students' drinking patterns and problems: Examining the effects of raising the purchase age. *Public Health Reports, 103*(6), 667-673.

Engs, R.C., & Hanson, D.J. (1989). Gender differences in drinking patterns and problems among college students: A review of the literature. *Journal of Alcohol and Drug Education, 35*(2), 36-47.

Geller, E.S. (1989). Applied behavior analysis and social marketing: An integration for environmental preservation. *Journal of Social Issues, 45,* 17-36.

Geller, E.S., & Glindemann, K.E. (February, 1996). *Intervening with fraternities to decrease alcohol abuse.* Final report for Grant # 5 R01 AA09604-02 from the National Institute on Alcohol Abuse and Alcoholism.

Geller, E.S., Kalsher, M.J., & Clarke, S.W. (1991). Beer versus mixed-drink consumption at university parties: A time and place for low alcohol alternatives. *Journal of Studies on Alcohol, 52,* 197-204.

Geller, E.S., Winett, R.A., & Everett, P.B. (1982). *Preserving the environment: New strategies for behavior change.* Elmsford, New York: Pergamon Press.

Glindemann, K.E., Geller, E.S., & Fortney, J.N. (1997). Self-esteem and alcohol impairment: A naturalistic study of college drinking behavior. Submitted for publication.

Glindemann, K.E., Geller, E.S., & Ludwig, T.D. (1996). Behavioral intentions and blood alcohol concentration: A relationship for prevention intervention. *Journal of Alcohol and Drug Education, 41*(2), 120-134.

Johnston, L.D. (1990). *Drug use, drinking and smoking: National survey results from high school, college and young adult populations, 1975-1988.* Washington, D.C.: National Institute on Drug Abuse.

Laurence, M.D., Snortum, J.R., & Zimring, F.E. (1988). *The social control of drinking and driving.* Chicago: University of Chicago Press.

Orcutt, J.D. (1993). Happy hour and social lubrication: Evidence on mood-setting rituals of drinking time. *Journal of Drug Issues, 23*(3), 389-407.

Orcutt, J.D., & Harvey, L.K. (1991). The temporal patterning of tension reduction: Stress and alcohol use on weekdays and weekends. *Journal of Studies on Alcohol, 52*(5), 415-424.

Perkins, H.W. (1992). Gender patterns in consequences of collegiate alcohol abuse: A 10-year study of trends in an undergraduate population. *Journal of Studies on Alcohol, 53,* 458-462.

Sleet, D.A., Wagenaar, A.C., & Waller, P.F. (1989). Drinking, driving, and health promotion. *Health Education Quarterly, 16*(3), 329-332.

Wechsler, H., Davenport, A., Dowdall, G., Moeykens, B., & Castillo, S. (1994). Health and behavioral consequences of binge drinking in college. *Journal of the American Medical Association, 272,* 1672-1677.

Identifying Potential
Drinking-Driving Recidivists:
Do Non-Obvious Indicators Help?

Thomas H. Nochajski

Research Institute on Addictions

William F. Wieczorek

Buffalo State College

SUMMARY. This study addressed two related questions concerning screening processes for convicted drinking-drivers: first, do these individuals falsify information to avoid detection; and second, do non-obvious indicators improve the ability to detect potential recidivists? Two samples of New York State Drinking Driver Program (DDP) participants were used. The first consisted of 1,592 first-time drinking-driving offenders who completed the Michigan Alcoholism Screening Test (MAST) and RIA Self Inventory (RIASI) screening instruments under confidential conditions. The second sample of 513 first-time offenders completed these instruments under normal screening conditions. The MAST contains 25 items that are directly associated with alcohol-related problems. In contrast, the RIASI contains 15 alcohol-related items associated with alcohol beliefs,

---

This research was a cooperative venture with the New York State Department of Motor Vehicles Division of Traffic Safety Services and was supported by the Governor's Traffic Safety Committee of New York State with funds from the National Highway Traffic Safety Administration.

[Haworth co-indexing entry note]: "Identifying Potential Drinking-Driving Recidivists: Do Non-Obvious Indicators Help?" Nochajski, Thomas H., and William F. Wieczorek. Co-published simultaneously in *Journal of Prevention & Intervention in the Community* (The Haworth Press, Inc.) Vol. 17, No. 1, 1998, pp. 69-83; and: *Preventing Drunk Driving* (ed: Elsie R. Shore, and Joseph R. Ferrari) The Haworth Press, Inc., 1998, pp. 69-83. Single or multiple copies of this article are available for a fee from The Haworth Document Delivery Service [1-800-342-9678, 9:00 a.m. - 5:00 p.m. (EST). E-mail address: getinfo@haworth.com].

family history for alcohol problems, and drinking practices, and 31 non-obvious or more distal items that reflect areas associated with alcohol or drug problems. Relative to the sample that completed the screening instruments under conditions of guaranteed confidentiality, the sample that completed the screening instruments under normal screening conditions showed reduced referral rates, lower scores on the MAST, and lower scores on the RIASI. In addition, the RIASI proved to be more effective at identifying potential recidivists than the MAST across both samples. The utility of including non-obvious indicators in the screening process is discussed. *[Article copies available for a fee from The Haworth Document Delivery Service: 1-800-342-9678. E-mail address: getinfo@haworth.com]*

INTRODUCTION

This study focused on the screening process of the New York State Drinking Driver Program (DDP). Screening procedures generally use measures that directly assess problems with alcohol and/ or drugs. One of the problems with alcohol-specific measures, like the Michigan Alcoholism Screening Test (MAST: Selzer, 1971) is that only individuals willing to identify themselves as having a problem are likely to be detected. Vingilis (1983) noted that DWI offenders may be unwilling to answer the direct questions truthfully, since they understand that by admitting to problems they will be mandated to treatment. Because of this falsification, individuals who are in the early stages of alcohol or drug problems, or those individuals who are trying to avoid detection will be missed (Babor, 1993; Saunders, Phic, & Kershaw, 1980). Since the literature indicates that appropriate treatment of drinking-drivers can result in reduced risk (Wells-Parker, Bangert-Drowns, McMillen, & Williams, 1995; Wieczorek, 1995), one result of the misidentification that may occur through the use of direct screening measures is increased drinking-driving recidivism and alcohol/drug-related crash rates.

The rationale for development of an instrument that uses non-obvious indicators for screening purposes, such as the RIA Self Inventory (RIASI: Nochajski, Miller, Augustino, & Kramer, 1995; Nochajski, Miller, Wieczorek, & Parks, 1993), is based in the literature that underscores the problems mentioned previously (Babor, Kranzler, & Lauerman, 1989; Miller & Windle, 1990). Specifically, the RIASI assesses a variety of proximal (current consumption, alcohol beliefs, preoccupation with alcohol, family history) and distal characteristics (hostility, sensation seeking, depression, anxiety, interpersonal competence, risky health behavior) that are highly correlated with alcohol or drug problems (Donovan & Marlatt, 1982; McMillen, Adams, Wells-Parker, Pang & Anderson, 1992; Oei & Jones, 1986; Parks, Nochajski, Wieczorek, & Miller, 1996; Pristach, Nochajski, Wieczorek, Miller, & Greene, 1991; Ross, Glaser, & Germanson, 1988; Windle & Miller, 1989). The use of distal or indirect measures for screening may help to identify individuals in the early stages of alcohol or drug problems and may also help circumvent some of the falsification that occurs in the drinking-driver population. While identification and referral of potential recidivists is not a guarantee of stopping continued drinking-driving, it does increase the likelihood that the behavior will be reduced (see Wells-Parker et al., 1995).

The current study compared psychometric properties of the RIASI and the MAST to identify recidivists across two samples of convicted drinking-drivers. Participants were from the New York State DDP. This program is a voluntary 16 hour seven-week educational program that is part of a secondary prevention process for convicted drinking-drivers. As an incentive, participants are offered a conditional license that allows them limited driving privileges. The primary target of this program is the first-time offender; however, second offenders, and sometimes third offenders, are eligible if the prior offenses occurred more than 5 years antecedent to the current offense. There are three basic functions of the DDP. The primary task is to educate the participant about the effects that alcohol and drugs have on his/her life. A secondary function is to screen for high-risk individuals and refer them for more thorough clinical assessments and treatment. Finally, the DDP monitors the participants to make sure all program requirements are fulfilled, including completion of alcohol/drug treatment if the participant is recommended for such treatment.

Two questions were addressed in this study. One question considered whether the DDP participants falsify information to avoid referral for clinical evaluation. A second question focused on whether inclusion of non-obvious indicators increased the effectiveness of the screening process, basically addressing whether the RIASI or MAST were more effective at identifying potential recidivists.

METHODS

Participants

1992 Statewide Survey Sample. One sample of participants (Sample 1) consisted of a subset of the 6,434 individuals that were part of a statewide survey of the DDPs in New York State (Nochajski, Miller, & Wieczorek, 1992). A total of 1,592 first-time offenders provided sufficient information for follow-up purposes and completed both the MAST and RIASI.

Comparisons were made between the included and excluded survey participants across demographic, drinking and drug-related characteristics. There were no differences in the gender makeup of the groups (84% males). However, in contrast to the included group ($M = 35.25$, $SD = 11.99$), the excluded group was slightly younger ($M = 33.95$, $SD = 11.08$), $t(2832) = 3.70$, $p < .001$. Furthermore, when compared to the included group (13.8%), the excluded group (17.2%) was more likely to have had prior treatment for alcohol and/or drug problems, χ^2 (1, $N = 5469$) = 9.26, $p < .005$. The excluded group (31.4%) was also more likely than the included group (27.4%) to have current problems with drugs other than alcohol, $\chi^2(1, N = 5063) = 8.18$, $p < .005$. Finally, the excluded group (26.8%) was more likely than the included group (22.5%) to drive after using drugs other than alcohol, χ^2 (1, $N = 5017) = 9.94$, $p < .005$. The included and excluded groups did not differ on any other characteristics.

1993 Erie County Sample. The second sample (Sample 2) consisted of 513 individuals who participated in the DDP in Erie County between January and October of 1993. The sample consisted primarily of males (81%), with a Mean age of 35 ($SD = 12.03$). These participants were administered both the MAST and RIASI as part of the screening process. During this time period some classes were administered the Mortimer-Filkins Questionnaire instead of the MAST. Since this study focused on the MAST and since the 1992 survey did not include the Mortimer-Filkins Questionnaire, these individuals were excluded from the current study. Comparison between the excluded and included group showed no differences for any demographic or drinking-related characteristics.

Procedure and Measures

1992 Statewide Survey Sample. The survey was voluntary and was conducted between the months of February and July of 1992. During that period, all participants in all DDP classes across the state were provided with survey questionnaires. Participants were guaranteed that their responses would not be shared with program instructors or directors. As part of the survey the participants were provided with consent forms and asked if they would be willing to provide their names and addresses for purposes of follow-up. The Diagnostic Interview Schedule (DIS) section for lifetime alcohol diagnoses (Robins, Helzer, Cotter, & Goldring, 1989), the Drug Abuse Screening Test (DAST: Skinner, 1982), drug use questions, the MAST, and a preliminary version of the RIASI were included in the survey. Since all repeat offenders are automatically referred for clinical evaluations, only first-time offenders were considered for the current study.

The initial version of the RIASI consisted of 45 items. Fifteen items included references to alcohol and for the purposes of the current study will be considered the drinking-related items. However, while they referenced alcohol, they did not address alcohol problems per se. The items related more to alcohol expectancies or beliefs about the effects of alcohol, family history, and drinking practices. The other thirty items addressed such areas as: aggression/hostility, sensation seeking, psychiatric distress (anxiety and depression), interpersonal competence, and risky health behavior. Scores for the instrument were derived by simply counting the number of responses indicative of a substance abuse problem. For this paper, separate scores were calculated for the drinking-related and non-drinking items, as well as for the total.

Driver abstracts were obtained for both samples from the Department of Motor Vehicles (DMV) in August of 1996. The resulting follow-up time period for the 1992 statewide sample ranged between 48 and 53 months, with a Mean of 51.3 (*SD* = 1.30) months. The DMV driver abstracts contained only the drinking-driving incidents that resulted in a conviction. Thus, recidivism is based on convictions, not arrests. A total of 186 individuals (12%) were subsequently convicted of a drinking-driving offense.

1993 Erie County Sample. A critical difference between the 1992 statewide survey sample and the 1993 Erie County sample was in how the screening instruments were administered. In contrast to the confidential conditions for the 1992 survey sample, the participants in this sample knew that responses would be viewed by DDP instructors and used for referral purposes. Thus, comparisons of referral rates based on MAST scores would provide some indication of the level of falsification that occurs in the DDP screening process.

The version of the MAST used with this sample was slightly different from that used with the statewide sample. The two versions had 24 items in common. Both did not include the drinking-driving question. The difference was in the content of the 25th item. The DDP version asked a question about alcohol detoxification, while the statewide survey asked a question about emotional problems due to drinking. Comparisons within each sample between the 24 and 25 item versions, showed that for both samples, one individual would have been missed at the more liberal cut point of 4 or more on the MAST. As a result, the decision was made to use the 25 items available in each respective sample.

A slightly modified version of the RIASI was used in this sample. Prior to implementation of this study, the initial forty-five item version was given to clinicians for their comment. The revised version used with this sample reflects the recommended changes. These included adding one item pertaining to social stability. Thus, the modified version contained 46 items, fifteen drinking-related items and thirty-one non-drinking items. The scoring system remained the same as for the initial version, a simple count of problem-directed responses. As with the initial version, scores were calculated for the drinking-related and non-drinking items, as well as for the total.

The 1993 Erie County sample had a follow-up period of between 32 and 42 months, with a Mean of 35.8 (*SD* = 2.61) months. Forty-one individuals from this sample were subsequently convicted of a drinking-driving offense (8%).

RESULTS

Comparison of Sample Characteristics

There were no age or gender differences across the samples. Recidivism rates for Sample 1 (3.9% and 7.1% for 12 and 24 months of follow-up, respectively) and Sample 2 (3.9% and 7.4% for 12 and 24-months of follow-up, respectively) also did not differ across common follow-up periods. However, Sample 1 ($M = 3.47$, $SD = 1.88$) had more traffic infractions listed on the driver abstract than Sample 2 ($M = 2.33$, $SD = 1.58$), t (1019) = 13.54, $p < .001$. Thus, while the two samples were generally equivalent in terms of age and gender, it appears that Sample 1 contained more high risk drivers than Sample 2.

Comparisons for Drinking-Related Characteristics

Since the drinking-related characteristics shown in Table 1 were part of the RIASI, any variations between the two samples were likely to be the result of the differences in the context under which the respondents completed the information. Sample 1 was more likely than Sample 2 to report a family history for alcohol or drug problems, χ^2 (1, $N = 2,102$) = 10.52, p < .005, and having a family member that was arrested for a DWI, χ^2 (1, $N = 2,095$) = 5.92, p < .05. There were also significant differences for current drinking, with Sample 1 reporting higher rates than Sample 2 for drinking 2 or more days per week, χ^2 (1, $N = 2,013$) = 22.29, p < .001; drinking 6 or more drinks at each drinking occasion, χ^2 (1, $N = 2,014$) = 8.66, p < .005; and spending \$20 or more per week on alcohol, χ^2 (1, $N = 1,956$) = 10.87, p < .005. In addition, individuals in Sample 1 were significantly more likely than individuals in Sample 2 to report drinking 15 or more drinks in one sitting, χ^2 (1, $N = 1,862$) = 20.44, p < .001. It is clear that the responses for the drinking-related items were diminished in Sample 2, where participants knew their answers would be used for referral purposes.

TABLE 1. Drinking-Related Comparisons Between the 1992 Statewide Sample and the 1993 Erie County Sample

Characteristics	Sample 1 1992 (n = 1,592)	Sample 2 1993 (n = 513)
Family history of alcohol/drug problems	37.2%	29.2%
Family member arrested for DWI	23.5%	18.6%
15 or more drinks in one drinking occasion	34.0%	22.9%
$20 or more per week on alcohol or drugs	38.3%	30.0%
Drink on 2 or more days per week	51.4%	39.2%
6 or more drinks per drinking occasion	31.4%	24.4%
When drinking, drink at more than one place	42.9%	38.4%
Score on RIA Self Inventory (RIASI)	10.54 (5.95)	8.32 (5.38)
Score on RIASI Drinking items	3.89 (2.86)	2.98 (2.56)
Score on RIASI Non-Drinking items	6.65 (3.62)	5.35 (3.54)
Count of positive responses on MAST	3.63 (3.82)	2.31 (2.65)
Weighted MAST score (Selzer)	6.22 (8.67)	3.22 (5.39)

Note: For all characteristics with means, standard deviations are in parentheses.

Also shown in Table 1 are the differences in the scores for the RIASI and MAST. As was found for the specific drinking-related items within the RIASI, Sample 1 also had higher scores than Sample 2 for the total RIASI, $t(947) = 7.82$, p < .001; the total of drinking-related items, $t(951) = 6.64$, p < .001; and the total of the non-drinking items, $t(951) = 7.02$, p < .001. Furthermore, when using the standard total score RIASI cutoff of 10 or more, the percent of individuals referred from Sample 2 (39.6%) was significantly lower than the percent that would have been referred from

Sample 1 (49.7%), χ^2 (1, N = 2,105) = 16.12, p < .001. Thus, even when using a screening instrument with non-obvious indicators, the referral rates were significantly diminished when respondents understood that their answers would be used by the DDP instructors for referral purposes.

Findings for the analyses with the MAST were similar to those for the RIASI. Scores on the MAST were significantly lower in Sample 2, whether the unitary, $t(1,243)$ = 8.31, p < .001, or the weighted method of scoring was used, $t(1,306)$ = 8.78, p < .001. In addition, when referral rates were compared for the unitary scoring procedure with a cutoff of 4 or more, the rates for Sample 2 (19.5%) were significantly reduced from those for Sample 1 (33%), χ^2 (1, N = 2,105) = 34.08, p < .001. Referral rates for the weighted scoring procedure using a cutoff of 5 or more showed the same trend, with the rates of referral for Sample 2 (22.6%) being significantly lower than those for Sample 1 (37.7%), χ^2 (1, N = 2,105) = 16.12, p < .001. Given this lower response rate on the MAST, and resulting lowered referral rates, it follows that detection of potential recidivists would be lessened. It should also be noted that while the rates of referral were diminished for the RIASI, they were still substantially higher than those for the MAST. This reinforces the need for using non-obvious or indirect methods when screening offenders.

Identification of Recidivists

There are two important measures of a screening test's performance: sensitivity (the proportion of individuals with the condition who are identified by the test) and specificity (the proportion of individuals without the condition who are identified as not having a problem by the screening test). The false positive rate (individuals identified as having a problem when in fact they do not) is the inverse of specificity and the false negative rate (individuals with a problem that are missed) is the inverse of sensitivity.

Table 2 shows the sensitivity (percent of identified recidivists) for various cut points on the MAST and RIASI. The interesting point from Table 2 is that the sensitivity for each of the respective instruments and respective cutoff points appeared to be relatively consistent across samples, even though the overall referral rates were reduced in Sample 2.

TABLE 2. Identification of Drinking-Driving Recidivists as a Function of the MAST and RIA Self Inventory (RIASI)

	% of Recidivists identified by each respective instrument	
	Sample 1 1992	Sample 2 1993
4 or more positive responses on MAST	39.8%	46.3%
5 or more positive responses on MAST	27.4%	26.8%
6 or more positive responses on MAST	24.2%	22.0%
Weighted Score on MAST–5 or more	42.5%	48.8%
10 or more positive responses on RIASI	57.0%	63.4%
9 or more positive responses on RIASI	67.2%	65.9%
3 or more drinking-related items from RIASI	67.7%	78.0%
6 or more non-drinking items from RIASI	66.7%	63.4%

For the MAST, whether unitary scoring with a cutoff of 4 positive responses or weighted scoring with a cutoff of 5 was used, less than 50% of the recidivists were identified regardless of which sample was being considered. This means that the MAST, with these more liberal scoring procedures, still had a false negative rate of over 50%. The RIASI reduced the false negative rate to between 22 and 43%, depending on the sample and scoring procedure. While the RIASI still missed a number of recidivists, it was markedly better than the MAST. In fact, the non-drinking items alone appeared to do a better job at identifying potential recidivists than the MAST.

Comparison of Instrument Sensitivities

These next set of analyses compared the sensitivities of the RIASI and MAST. Initially, analyses were performed separately for each sample. However, since the findings for the two samples showed similar patterns, all recidivists were combined. Table 3 shows the number of recidivists that were correctly identified by each screening procedure. The RIASI total score, with a cutoff of 10 or more, performed significantly better than the MAST, whether the unitary scoring procedure, $\chi^2(1, N = 227) = 22.22$, p < .0001, or the weighted scoring procedure was used, $\chi^2(1, N = 227) = 14.42$, p < .001. Differences between the RIASI and MAST were even more noticeable when a cutoff of 9 was used for the RIASI, $\chi^2(1, N = 227) = 44.85$, p < .0001 and $\chi^2(1, N = 227) = 33.38$, p < .0001, for the unitary and weighted MAST scoring procedures, respectively. The score for the drinking-related items from the RIASI also was superior to the MAST, unitary, $\chi^2(1, N = 227) = 41.38$, p < .0001, and weighted scoring procedures, $\chi^2(1, N = 227) = 32.76$, p < .0001. Finally, even the non-drinking items by themselves were superior to the MAST at identifying recidivists, $\chi^2(1, N = 227) = 36.01$, and p < .0001 $\chi^2(1, N = 227) = 26.94$, p < .0001 RIASI for the unitary and weighted scoring procedures, respectively. These results indicate that use of non-obvious indicators can substantially increase the ability to detect recidivists. Even alcohol-related questions that are non-problem oriented can increase the ability to detect recidivists.

DISCUSSION

The results for the comparisons between samples indicate that drinking-drivers do have a tendency to diminish responses on screening instruments. Comparison of referral rates between the statewide and Erie County samples also reflected this tendency to diminish responses. Given that the reason for the screening process is not just to reduce continued drinking-driving, but also to reduce problem drinking/drug use, the diminished response rates and resulting diminished referral rates are a concern. For secondary prevention to be successful, the high-risk individuals need to be correctly identified so they can be exposed to the proper types of interventions. This is particularly important in light of the fact that 60% of the statewide sample would have qualified for some type of lifetime DSM-III-R alcohol diagnosis. Within the 1993 Erie County sample, referral rates for the MAST ranged between 8 and 23%, while for the RIASI they ranged between 40 and 53%, depending

TABLE 3. Comparison of Sensitivities for the MAST and RIASI

		Number of Recidivists within each category	
		MAST < 4	MAST ≥ 4
RIASI	< 10	82	13
	≥ 10	52	80
RIASI	<9	67	8
	≥ 9	67	85
RIASI Drinking Items	< 3	60	13
	≥ 3	74	80
RIASI Non-Drinking Items	< 6	68	12
	≥ 6	66	81
		Weighted MAST < 5	Weighted MAST ≥ 5
RIASI	< 10	76	19
	≥ 10	52	80
RIASI	< 9	61	14
	≥ 9	67	85
RIASI Drinking Items	< 3	56	17
	≥ 3	72	82
RIASI Non-Drinking Items	< 6	63	17
	≥ 6	65	82

on the scoring process used. This underscores the need for screening procedures that use indirect methods to detect potential problem drinkers/drug users in the drinking-driving population.

Furthermore, Nochajski et al. (1995) found that the RIASI was better than the MAST at identifying problem drinkers. Non-obvious indicators in the RIASI helped reduce the number of false negatives substantially, from 42% to 18%, while not significantly increasing the number of false positives (19% as compared to 25%, on the MAST). This indicates that the ability to detect problem individuals can be greatly enhanced by inclusion of non-obvious indicators. Finally, since the false positive rates remain relatively low, this improvement can occur without overburdening the assessment and treatment systems.

The second focus of this study was on the relative effectiveness of the MAST and RIASI for identifying potential recidivists. Results for the comparisons show the RIASI as having a greater ability than the MAST to detect potential recidivists. In fact, the non-obvious indicators by themselves were able to identify more potential recidivists than the MAST, regardless of the scoring procedure used with the MAST. The implications from these findings are that recidivism of drinking-driving offenders may not be just a factor of alcohol-related problems, but more associated with a general deviance construct that includes heavy drinking, drug use, and risk taking. Concentration of screening efforts on alcohol-related problems may miss many individuals that are at high-risk for recidivism. The results of this study emphasize the need for screening and assessment devices that are not just focused on alcohol-related problems, providing further support for an instrument such as the RIASI to screen drinking-drivers.

Identification of factors that are associated with problem drinking, problem drug use, and DWI recidivism are important because they can lead to early recognition of potential high-risk individuals. By identifying these individuals at the point of their first arrest, measures can be taken to prevent continued problem drinking/drug use behavior. Furthermore, the identification of specific problem areas could lead to a better understanding of the causes of problem drinking/drug use and/or recidivism for that individual, which could then lead to development of interventions that are appropriate for these problems. Channeling the individuals into appropriate interventions should reduce problem drinking/drug use, and alcohol-related crashes and fatality rates.

The results for this study are specific to the DDP population. Given the method used in determining the cutoff for the RIASI, extension of its use to other populations would need to include investigation of baseline rates for alcohol and/or drug problems within that population. Currently, the RIASI is being pilot tested with samples of convicted drinking-drivers on probation, with plans to extend this to other criminal justice populations. In addition, work continues on the development of subscales that may help improve the efficiency of the RIASI and assist evaluators and treatment providers.

REFERENCES

Babor, T. F. (1993). Alcohol and drug use history, patterns and problems. In B. J. Rounsaville, F. M. Tims, & A. M. Horton, Jr. (Eds.), *Diagnostic source book on drug abuse research and treatment* (pp. 319-334). Rockville, MD: U.S. Department of Health and Human Services, National Institute on Drug Abuse.

Babor, T. F., Kranzler, H. R., & Lauerman, R.J. (1989). Early detection of harmful alcohol consumption: Comparison of clinical, laboratory, and self-report screening procedures. *Addictive Behaviors, 14,* 139-157.

Donovan, D. M., & Marlatt, G. A. (1982). Personality subtypes among driving-while-intoxicated offenders: Relationship to drinking behavior and driving risk. *Journal of Consulting and Clinical Psychology, 50,* 241-249.

Miller, B. A., & Windle, M. (1990). Alcoholism, problem drinking, and driving while impaired. In R. J. Wilson & R. E. Mann (Eds.), *Drinking and driving* (pp. 68-95). New York: Guilford Press.

McMillen, D.L., Adams, M.S., Wells-Parker, E., Pang, M.G., & Anderson, B.J. (1992). Personality traits and behaviors of alcohol-impaired drivers: A comparison of first and multiple offenders. *Addictive Behaviors, 17,* 407-414.

Nochajski, T. H., Miller, B. A., Augustino, D. K., & Kramer, R. (1995). Use of non-obvious indicators for screening of DWI offenders. In C. N. Kloeden & A. J. McLean (Eds.), *Alcohol, drugs and traffic safety-T95* (pp. 449-454). Adelaide: University of Adelaide.

Nochajski, T. H., Miller, B. A., & Wieczorek, W. F. (1992, October). The New York State drinking-driver program screening project. *Drinking, Drugs, & Driving Research Note, 92-2.*

Nochajski, T. H., Miller, B. A., Wieczorek, W. F., & Parks, K. A. (1993, June). *The utility of non-obvious indicators for screening of DWI offenders.* Paper presented at the annual meeting of the Research Society on Alcoholism, San Antonio, TX.

Oei, T. P., & Jones, R. (1986). Alcohol-related expectancies: Have they a role in the understanding and treatment of problem drinking? *Advances in Alcohol & Substance Abuse, 6*(1), 89-105.

Parks, K.A., Nochajski, T. H., Wieczorek, W. F., & Miller, B. A. (1996). Assessing alcohol problems in female DWI offenders. *Alcoholism: Clinical and Experimental Research, 20*(3), 434-439.

Pristach, E. A., Nochajski, T. H., Wieczorek, W. F., Miller, B. A., & Greene, B. (1991). Psychiatric symptoms and DWI offenders. In H. Kalant, J. M. Khana, & Y. Israel (Eds.), *Advances in biomedical alcohol research* (pp. 493-496). Oxford, England: Pergamon Press.

Robins, L., Helzer, J., Cotter, L., & Goldring, E. (1989). *NIMH diagnostic schedule: Version III revised (DIS-III-R)*. St. Louis, MO: Washington University.

Ross, H. E., Glaser, F. B., & Germanson, T. (1988). The prevalence of psychiatric disorders in patients with alcohol and other drug problems. *Archives of General Psychiatry, 45,* 1023-1031.

Saunders, W. M., Phic, M., & Kershaw, P. W. (1980). Screening tests for alcoholism–Findings from a community study. *British Journal of Addiction, 75,* 37-41.

Selzer, M. L. (1971). The Michigan Alcoholism Screening Test: The Quest for a new diagnostic instrument. *American Journal of Psychiatry, 127*(12), 89-94.

Skinner, H. A. (1982). The Drug Abuse Screening Test. *Addictive Behaviors, 7,* 363-371.

Vingilis, E. (1983). Drinking drivers and alcoholics: Are they from the same population? In R. G. Smart, F. B. Glaser, Y. Israel, H. Kalant, R. E. Popham, & W. Schmidt (Eds.), *Research advances in alcohol and drug problems: Vol. 7* (pp. 299-342). New York: Plenum Press.

Wells-Parker, E., Bangert-Drowns, R., McMillen, R., & Williams, M. (1995). Final results from a meta-analysis of remedial interventions with drink/drive offenders. *Addiction, 90,* 907-926.

Wieczorek, W. F. (1995). The role of treatment in reducing alcohol-related accidents involving DWI offenders. In R. R. Watson (Ed.), *Drug and alcohol abuse reviews* (pp. 105-129). Totowa, NJ: Humana Press, Inc.

Windle, M., & Miller, B. A. (1989). Alcoholism and depressive symptomatology among convicted DWI men and women. *Journal of Studies on Alcohol, 50*(5), 406-413.

Index

AA. *See* Alcoholics Anonymous
Adebayo, A., 46
advertising, reaching young adults
    through, 7
African Americans, 27. *See also* race
age, influence on intervention
    efforts, 46
Alberta (Canada)
    drunk driving recidivism study in,
      35
    ignition interlock program
      modifications, 36-41
alcohol
    abuse among young adults, 56
    accidents related to (*See* traffic
      accidents)
    deaths related to (*See* traffic
      fatalities)
    relationship between availability
      and drunk driving, 16,22-24
    resistance to change among
      abusers of, 40
Alcoholics Anonymous (AA), 35
alcohol interlock. *See* ignition
    interlock devices and
    programs
Arfken, C. L., 64,66

BAC. *See* blood alcohol
    concentration
behavior change, stage paradigm
    model of, 40
Beirness, D. J., 35
Bell, A., 40
binge drinking, 10,56
blood alcohol concentration (BAC)
    feedback study, 55,57-60
    gender differences, 61-63,65

link to traffic fatalities, 56
brain injuries, 39
brewers, designated driver programs, 2
Brigham, T. A., 2,4

California, supervision programs, 33
Campbell, D. T., 5
Castillo, S., 56
ceiling-effect hypothesis, 6,7
Change Readiness Theory, 37
change resistance, alcohol offenders
    and, 40
CNN (cable TV channel), 8
cocaine use, compared to alcohol
    use, 56
college students. *See* young adults
competence, intervention perceived
    as a threat to, 45,47-52
confrontation, influence on
    intervention efforts, 51-52

Davenport, A., 56
DeJong, W., 2
designated driver, definition, 1,2
designated driving
    efforts to increase, 2-11
    how to measure, 11
    normalizing the practice of, 13
    reasons to promote, 12
    theory, criticism of, 2,10
deterrence, as a method to control
    recidivism, 32
Dowdall, G., 56
drinking, context and intervention,
    16,17
driver's license reinstatement
    statistics, 33,36

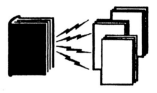

Haworth
DOCUMENT DELIVERY
SERVICE

This valuable service provides a single-article order form for any article from a Haworth journal.

- *Time Saving:* No running around from library to library to find a specific article.
- *Cost Effective:* All costs are kept down to a minimum.
- *Fast Delivery:* Choose from several options, including same-day FAX.
- *No Copyright Hassles:* You will be supplied by the original publisher.
- *Easy Payment:* Choose from several easy payment methods.

Open Accounts Welcome for . . .
- Library Interlibrary Loan Departments
- Library Network/Consortia Wishing to Provide Single-Article Services
- Indexing/Abstracting Services with Single Article Provision Services
- Document Provision Brokers and Freelance Information Service Providers

---

MAIL or *FAX* THIS ENTIRE ORDER FORM TO:

Haworth Document Delivery Service
The Haworth Press, Inc.
10 Alice Street
Binghamton, NY 13904-1580

or FAX: 1-800-895-0582
or CALL: 1-800-342-9678
9am-5pm EST

PLEASE SEND ME PHOTOCOPIES OF THE FOLLOWING SINGLE ARTICLES:

1) Journal Title: _____
   Vol/Issue/Year: _____ Starting & Ending Pages: _____
   Article Title: _____

2) Journal Title: _____
   Vol/Issue/Year: _____ Starting & Ending Pages: _____
   Article Title: _____

3) Journal Title: _____
   Vol/Issue/Year: _____ Starting & Ending Pages: _____
   Article Title: _____

4) Journal Title: _____
   Vol/Issue/Year: _____ Starting & Ending Pages: _____
   Article Title: _____

(See other side for Costs and Payment Information)

COSTS: Please figure your cost to order quality copies of an article.

1. Set-up charge per article: $8.00

    ($8.00 × number of separate articles)   _____

2. Photocopying charge for each article:

    1-10 pages: $1.00   _____

    11-19 pages: $3.00   _____

    20-29 pages: $5.00   _____

    30+ pages: $2.00/10 pages   _____

3. Flexicover (optional): $2.00/article   _____

4. Postage & Handling: US: $1.00 for the first article/

    $.50 each additional article   _____

    Federal Express: $25.00   _____

    Outside US: $2.00 for first article/

    $.50 each additional article_____

5. Same-day FAX service: $.35 per page   _____

                                 GRAND TOTAL: _____

METHOD OF PAYMENT: (please check one)

❑ Check enclosed   ❑ Please ship and bill. PO # _____
    (sorry we can ship and bill to bookstores only! All others must pre-pay)

❑ Charge to my credit card: ❑ Visa; ❑ MasterCard; ❑ Discover;
                                      ❑ American Express;

Account Number:_____ Expiration date:_____

Signature: *X*_____

Name: _____ Institution: _____

Address: _____

_____

City: _____ State:_____ Zip:_____

Phone Number: _____ FAX Number: _____

MAIL or *FAX* THIS ENTIRE ORDER FORM TO:

Haworth Document Delivery Service	**or FAX:** 1-800-895-0582
The Haworth Press, Inc.	**or CALL:** 1-800-342-9678
10 Alice Street	9am-5pm EST)
Binghamton, NY 13904-1580	